NEWSMEN
& NATIONAL DEFENSE

Related Titles and Other AUSA Books:

Alexander & Latter	TERRORISM & THE MEDIA: DILEMMAS FOR GOVERNMENT, JOURNALISTS & THE PUBLIC
Alexander & Picard	IN THE CAMERA'S EYE: NEWS COVERAGE OF TERRORIST EVENTS
Matthews & Brown	ASSESSING THE VIETNAM WAR
Matthews & Brown	THE PARAMETERS OF WAR
Matthews & Brown	THE PARAMETERS OF MILITARY ETHICS
Matthews & Brown	THE CHALLENGE OF MILITARY LEADERSHIP

Related Journals*

Armed Forces Journal International
Defense Analysis
Survival

* Sample copies available upon request

AN AUSA BOOK

NEWSMEN & NATIONAL DEFENSE

Is Conflict Inevitable?

Edited by

Lloyd J. Matthews

Introduction by

Peter Braestrup

Published under the
auspices of the U.S.
Army War College
Foundation, Inc.

Selected by the Institute
of Land Warfare,
Association of
the U.S. Army

BRASSEY'S (US), INC.
A Division of Maxwell Macmillan, Inc.

Washington • New York • London • Oxford • Beijing
Frankfurt • São Paulo • Sydney • Tokyo • Toronto

Copyright © 1991 Brassey's (US), Inc.

Editorial Offices
Brassey's (US), Inc.
8000 Westpark Drive, 1st Floor,
McLean, Virginia 22102

Orders
Attn: Brassey's Order Dept., Macmillan Publishing Co.,
100 Front Street, Box 500, Riverside, New Jersey 08075

Brassey's (US), Inc., books are available at special discounts
for bulk purchases for sales promotions, premiums,
fund-raising, or educational use through the Special Sales
Director, Macmillan Publishing Company, 866 Third Avenue,
New York, NY 10022.

Library of Congress Cataloging-in-Publication Data

Newsmen & national defense : is conflict inevitable? / edited by
Lloyd J. Matthews ; introduction by Peter Braestrup.
    p.   cm. — (An AUSA book)
   "Selected by the Institute of Land Warfare, Association of
the U.S. Army."
   "Published under the auspices of the U.S. Army War
College Foundation, Inc."
   ISBN 0-08-040585-1 (hardcover)   0-08-041065-0 (softcover)
   1. Armed Forces and mass media—United States. 2. United
States—National security. 3. Freedom of information—United
States. I. Matthews, Lloyd J. II. Institute of Land Warfare
(Association of the United States Army) III. Title: Newsmen
and national defense. IV. Series: AUSA Institute of Land
Warfare book.
P96.A752U56   1991
070.4'49355'00973—dc20
                            91-7478
                              CIP

British Library Cataloguing in Publication Data

Newsmen & national defense : is conflict inevitable ?
   1. War. Role of media
   I. Matthews, Lloyd J.
   070.44935502

Printed in the United States of America
10 9 8 7 6 5 4 3 2 1

An AUSA Book

The Association of the United States Army, or AUSA, was founded in 1950 as a not-for-profit organization dedicated to education concerning the role of the U.S. Army, to providing material for military professional development, and to the promotion of proper recognition and appreciation of the profession of arms. Its constituencies include those who serve in the Army today, including Army National Guard, Army Reserve, and Army civilians, and the retirees and veterans who have served in the past, and all their families. A large number of public-minded citizens and business leaders are also an important constituency. The Association seeks to educate the public, elected and appointed officials, and leaders of defense industry on crucial issues involving the adequacy of our national defense, particularly those issues affecting land warfare.

In 1988 AUSA established within its existing organization a new entity known as the Institute of Land Warfare. Its purpose is to extend the educational work of AUSA by promoting scholarly publications, to include books, monographs, and essays on key defense issues, as well as workshops and symposia. Among the volumes chosen for designation as "An AUSA Institute of Land Warfare Book" are both new texts and reprints of titles of enduring value that are no longer in print. Topics include history, policy issues, strategy, and tactics. Publication as an AUSA Book does not indicate that the Association of the United States Army and the publisher agree with everything in the book, but does suggest that the AUSA and the publisher believe this book will stimulate the thinking of AUSA members and others concerned about important issues.

Contents

Preface

The Constitution signed by the nation's founders on 17 September 1787 did an eminently sensible thing by providing for the nation's defense: "The Congress shall have the power to . . . provide for the common defense . . . to declare war . . . to make rules for the government and regulation of the land and naval forces" (Article I, Section 8); "the President shall be commander in chief of the Army and Navy" (Article II, Section 2). Amending the Constitution on 15 December 1791 was the Bill of Rights, which also did an eminently sensible thing by guaranteeing the right of citizens to speak out: "Congress shall make no law . . . abridging the freedom of speech or of the press" (Article I).

The copresence of these two eminently sensible provisions in our Constitution has not, however, led to their harmonious coexistence, and the reasons are not hard to find. War attracts two varieties of men—the soldier who prosecutes it and the newsman who reports it. The soldier finds that operational security is an absolute condition for the successful prosecution of war; the newsman finds that operational security interferes with what he regards as his absolute right to report that war. And so the argument was born, an argument that continues to the present day and an argument, incidentally, that is inherent in any form of liberal democratic governance.

Ironically, our fledgling nation had begun to feel the impress of this clash of perspectives well before the argument became constitutionally ordained. In the spring of 1777, upon finding reports in New York newspapers that he felt undermined the war effort against England, an exasperated General George Washington fired off this missive: "It is much to be wished that our printers were more discreet in many of their publications. We see in almost every paper proclamations or accounts transmitted by the enemy of an injurious nature." Hardly a quarter of a century later, in 1809, the English were having similar problems. The Duke of Wellington lamented: "In some instances the English newspapers have accurately stated not only the regiments occupying a position, but the number of men fit for duty of which each regiment was composed; and this intelligence must have reached the enemy at the same time as it did me, at a moment at which it was most important that he should not receive it."

General William Tecumseh Sherman, during the American Civil War, expressed his animus against the press in some of the most colorfully vitriolic language ever recorded. In 1864, having heard a rumor that three reporters with the Union Army of the Tennessee had been captured by the rebels and executed, he rejoined: "Good! Now we'll have news from hell before breakfast!" During Sherman's march through Georgia, *New York Herald* correspondent DeBow Randolph Keim discovered that Union intelligence officials had successfully decrypted the Confederate signal flag code employed from mountain towers to transmit details of the Union advance. He reported this news in the *Herald* on 23 June 1864, and Sherman was livid. (This is the same Debow Keim, mind you, who had once boasted to colleagues that he didn't read Shakespeare for fear it would contaminate his writing style.) The complaints of Washington and Sherman comprise a refrain heard down through the centuries, wherever wars are fought by democratic polities.

Obviously, newsmen have their side of the story. They can claim, justly, that reporters have shared with soldiers the dangers and privations of war. In one of the more interesting footnotes of history, Major Marcus A. Reno, in his after-action report on Custer's last stand on the Little Big Horn in 1876, reported that the 204 bodies buried included that of Mark H. Kellogg, a correspondent for the *New York Herald.* In the Vietnam War, Phillip Knightley reports that 45 correspondents were killed and 18 recorded as missing. Knightley tells the story of United Press photographer Charlie Eggleston who, enraged at a fatal ambush of five of his colleagues in Cholon in May 1968, "took a weapon and announced that he was going out on a mission of revenge. He, too, was shot dead, but, as the story in Saigon went, not before he had first killed three Vietcong."

There is ample testimony to instances of journalistic self-regulation, where newsmen possessing compromising operational information voluntarily suppressed or deferred publication. A case in point is the news media's withholding from publication information potentially harmful to Marine Lieutenant Colonel William R. Higgins when he was captured by terrorists in Lebanon in 1987. The soldier worries whether journalistic voluntarism is a sufficiently strong mechanism upon which to hazard the lives of soldiers and the nation's military fortunes, especially in view of the highly competitive nature of the news business. The newsman worries whether any departure from the principle of voluntarism will not inevitably lead to externally imposed censorship.

But the more basic point to be made in behalf of war reporting by newsmen lies in the homely truism that for democracy to work it must have an informed electorate. War is quite simply the most seismic activity in which a society can engage. Since the ultimate decisions on the conduct of war rest with the people, it follows with syllogistic certainty that democracies must discover means to arm the people with the facts necessary for informed judgment. A free and independent press, protected by constitutional guarantees, is the only yet-devised means of assuring that the people have access to the needed sources of information.

In reconciling the divergent claims of soldier and newsman, it is essential that each camp gain a full appreciation of the legitimate claims of the other and swallow a generous dose of empathy. A prominent contemporary correspondent and First Amendment absolutist, who spoke at the Naval War College's Military-Media Conference at Newport, Rhode Island, in November 1986, remarked informally during a break that if the United States were at war with the Soviet Union and he learned the date and time of sailing of a U.S. troopship, he would feel obliged to publish the information. For a reporter to believe this, much less to say it to a uniformed audience, was unspeakably dopey. He later softened his stance with the explanation that if *he* knew when the ship was sailing then the Soviets could be assumed to know it too. But this rationale hardly mollified the outraged servicemen among his listeners.

Nor is the soldier himself without sin in matters of interprofessional tact and understanding. Bernard Weisberger has chronicled the following telling episode occurring during Sherman's march across Georgia:

> A staff officer hotly rebuked an inquisitive reporter and told him to go to Washington, where the news would filter from official channels suitably purified. Told that the country was eager for information, the officer bellowed: "What the hell do we care about the country?" The remark was reported by the chastised interviewer.

Any staff officer today who displayed this sort of vacancy of mind would, we can be sure, find himself instantly sacked.

The fact that this is so suggests that over the last one and a quarter centuries we have managed to bridge somewhat the yawning gulf that at one time separated the soldier and the newsman. It is difficult to imagine, for example, that any senior field commander today could long remain in his position who waged a vituperative and prolonged public skirmish with the news media in the manner of General Sherman. And it is equally unlikely that newsmen covering an American shooting war today would be guilty of as many blatant and damaging security breaches as were committed by reporters during the Civil War. Certainly the markedly successful example of the press pool assembled for Operation Desert Shield and dispatched to Saudi Arabia in August 1990 gives grounds for optimism. Cooperation between military officials and press pool members was, by all accounts, exemplary.

But bridges, like all human artifacts, are subject to the corrosive effects of time and circumstance. They must be continually tended, refurbished, and even replaced in a never-ending process of renewal. The comparatively idyllic relations enjoyed between the two camps during World War II gave no foreglimpse of the utter breakdown between them that would occur during the latter part of the Vietnam War. By the same token, the glow of comity we witnessed during Desert Shield largely evaporated during Operation Desert Storm, the action to liberate Kuwait.

In this connection, Secretary of Defense Richard Cheney's relief of Air Force Chief of Staff General Michael Dugan in September 1990 over the latter's frank public discussion of U.S. plans for air attacks against Iraq has led to doleful warnings that the Pentagon might as a consequence "rebuild the wall between the media and the military" that was erected during the Vietnam War. This is a misleading way to frame the problem, however, because General Dugan's misfortune had nothing to do with the traditional animosity between soldier and newsman. General Dugan's decision to go public was calculated on his part, and so far as we may judge his views were reported in the press fairly and accurately. The Dugan case may illustrate a degree of contention between the soldier and his civilian masters, but not between the soldier and the news media.

The essays contained in the present collection portray the structurally embedded tension between the soldier and the press as it has expressed itself at several important junctures over our nation's history. Two reciprocal principles would seem to emerge from the discussions. First, the soldier is obligated to provide means, consistent with operational security and effectiveness, whereby the newsman is enabled to observe and accurately report the military and the wars it fights. Second, in determining the news he will report, the newsman in turn is obligated to respect the safety of the soldier and his prospects for success on the battlefield. These two principles imply a corollary, namely, that the two sides can best fulfill their obligations to each other by achieving maximum mutual understanding. By following such principles, the knight and the newsman may never be able to dissolve entirely the gulf that separates them, but they should be able to maintain sufficient safe crossings to vindicate the Constitutional framers' confidence that our right to defend ourselves could successfully coexist with our right to speak to ourselves.

Colonel Lloyd J. Matthews, U.S. Army (Ret.)
Carlisle Barracks, Pennsylvania

Acknowledgments

The acknowledgments in books are often slighted by readers. This would be a pity in the case of the present work, which is a product of numerous hands scarcely divinable from the brief byline on the title page.

We begin with the commandant of the U.S. Army War College, Major General Paul G. Cerjan, who has labored indefatigably to promote a climate of free intellectual inquiry at the War College. In the seminar rooms, from the lecture podiums, and on the pages of the College journal *Parameters*, the burning issues of the contemporary security landscape are confronted squarely and debated to the last word. Throughout this effort, the commandant has been ably seconded by the director of academic affairs, Colonel David A. Bouton, who has remained firmly wed to the principle that the most enlightened policy can precipitate only from the most unflinching inquiry.

The core and essence of the book consist of the eleven essays, all but two of which appeared originally in *Parameters*. The two exceptions are Joseph H. Ewing's piece on the new Sherman letters, which was first published in *American Heritage*, and Fred S. Hoffman's report to the assistant secretary of defense for public affairs on the Panamanian press pool. It is the individual authors of the assembled essays whom we would thank most warmly. They have ventured publicly into the hotly contentious thicket of media-military relations without mincing words; we thank them for their courage and candor. They have built bridges rather than widening the gulf; we thank them for their good offices.

The direct ministrations of three Very Important Persons also deserve to be recorded. First is Colonel LeRoy Strong (U.S. Army Ret.), the War College's friend, benefactor, and *éminence grise* for nearly 23 years, most recently in his capacity as executive director of the Army War College Foundation, Inc., which sponsored publication of this book. Second is Mr. Gregory N. Todd, the associate editor of *Parameters*, whose editorial wizardry inheres in virtually every line throughout. Last is Mrs. Phyllis M. Stouffer, *Parameters'* editorial assistant, whose dextrous fingers, willing hands, nimble brain, and warm smile caused so many barriers to melt in a trice and so many loose parts to leap magically into place.

Introduction

Not quite a month after the Iraqis overran Kuwait and three weeks after George Bush dispatched the first American ground troops to Saudia Arabia as part of Operation Desert Shield, there came a loud complaint from Murray Gartner, president of NBC News. On the Op-Ed Page of the *Wall Street Journal* (30 August 1990) he wrote:

> Here's something you should know about that war [sic] that's going on in the Gulf: much of the news that you read or hear or see is being censored . . . there is no excuse for this kind of censorship [which] exceeds even the most stringent censorship of World War II.

Gartner, a respected ex-newspaperman but a stranger to war reporting, was deploring the ground rules laid down for journalists by the U.S. command in Saudi Arabia. The rules said, in effect, "You don't tell the foe the unit designations, locations, numbers, and future dispositions of U.S. forces." Journalists covering Operation Desert Shield were largely limited to guided tours of selected U.S. field units; and on occasion, Gartner noted, television crews were forbidden to film certain military installations. "The press was shut out of Grenada," he wrote, "cooped up in Panama, and put on the late plane [carrying the Pentagon press pool] into Saudi Arabia." Once again, he concluded, the Pentagon had no use for the "facts."

Like many journalists (and other Americans) at the beginning of the 1990s, Gartner had a hazy memory of past wars. He did not recall similar rules in effect in Vietnam or outright field censorship during the Korean conflict and World War II. Nor did he seem to understand the enemy threat to U.S. forces: not an outnumbered, irresolute militia (Grenada, Panama) or outgunned albeit tenacious light infantry (Vietnam), but a modern army with armor, artillery, aircraft, missiles, and some sizable elite units (the Republican Guards), enjoying numerical superiority and offensive capability. Some prudence on the part of the U.S. Persian Gulf commanders was in order.

What Gartner also seemed to overlook was that reporters, operating within the ground rules in Washington and Saudi Arabia, had managed to convey the essential "facts" to the American public. These facts were that (1) American Marines, Army airborne units, Navy ships, and Air Force combat aircraft were deploying in the largest U.S. overseas expedition since Vietnam; (2) they faced a dangerous well-equipped adversary in desert terrain under austere (by U.S. peacetime standards) conditions; (3) their local allies were helping out; (4) the Americans were new to the desert and to possible combat; and (5) they were getting into a solid defensive posture (despite delays in the arrival of Army armored units), with allied Arab forces up front. Much more detail became known thereafter, but during the month of August 1990, during the initial buildup, the American public was not being kept in the dark.

The real reason for Gartner's ire may have been this: at great expense, NBC and the other major networks were maintaining dozens of technicians, producers, cameramen, and reporters in Saudia Arabia—and the results in the late summer of 1990, in the absence of combat, were not compelling "visuals." Operation Desert Shield, during its first month at least, simply did not provide the kind of drama that television news, like television generally, dotes on. Indeed, the fast-fast-fast snippets of film on the evening programs showed once again the increasing poverty of the TV news vocabulary—Air Force C-141 transports landing, Marine jet fighters taking off, Navy ships steaming through the Suez Canal, Army Sheridan tanks maneuvering (on cue) as camels and Bedouins amble by, G.I.s in desert camouflage uniforms drinking water and complaining about the heat. Television news, as it has evolved, favors a clear story line, smoke, flame, emotion, spectacle. The complexities of the Persian Gulf buildup did not lend themselves to nine-second sound bites or the pontifications of anchormen flown to Amman or Riyadh for the occasion.

To the press and to the military alike, the coverage of Operation Desert Shield posed some other problems. First, there were on hand, by early September, more than 450 "journalists"—actually, the lion's share were technicians and other members of television crews, not reporters—from America and abroad. This was a larger contingent than was deployed to Vietnam. The Saudis, always wary of foreigners, issued visas for brief sojourns only. So there was much coming and going, and overworked military public affairs officers had to cope with constant waves of clamoring newcomers. Second, the journalists flying in from America, even those from the Big League, were mostly men (and women) under 40 and unfamiliar with the military and its ways. It was 15 years since Hanoi "liberated" South Vietnam and almost two decades since the Pentagon abandoned the draft. The ensuing divorce between the U.S. military and U.S. society, particularly the young college-educated segment of that society, was nowhere more evident than in the ranks of journalism. (In the fall of 1990, for example, only two of the 22 reporters in the Washington bureau of the *Wall Street Journal* had ever been in uniform.) The Pentagon, especially after the ill feeling aroused by the initial exclusion of reporters from the Grenada invasion of 1983, had made some effort to educate officers on the necessary role of the press in democratic America. No comparable effort was made in journalism schools or in mid-career programs for newspeople to educate reporters about the military; news coverage of the peacetime military during the 1980s focused heavily on Pentagon budgets, (costly) new weaponry, and the prospects for a post–Cold War "peace dividend."

So the Persian Gulf crisis, like the Grenada invasion, once again caught the military and the media in what might be best described as a clash of cultures. And most of the essays in this book, to some degree, reflect this clash.

The world of the soldier is not the world of the journalist. Military ideals center on the words "duty, honor, country." The military leader, as Morris Janowitz has observed, is "an officer and a gentleman." He is a member of a hierarchy, with a clear order of rank and with a defined career ladder. He must, of necessity, be a team player, who may disagree with his superiors but, after offering his arguments, must carry out their orders. If he finds advancement blocked or his superiors unbearable, he cannot easily change jobs; he may have to leave the service. Particularly in peacetime, in order to succeed he must avoid professional embarrassment. Further, he must deal with a myriad of people problems, red tape, and petty detail. If he is a field commander, he must learn how to motivate and lead ordinary men, using as his prime tools unit pride and cohesion.

In wartime, the commander faces the real test. He must exhibit confidence, know the capabilities of his men and their equipment, act decisively on insufficient information, carry out the mission, and in part trust to luck—and he must do all of this in the organized chaos of battle. In the current American context, he must prevail over the foe while losing as few men as possible, and killing as few civilians as possible. Failure means not only personal disgrace but the futile deaths of his men and possibly the defeat of his country.

The great majority of officers, of course, do not face the real test: they are technicians, staff officers, and managers of the vast support system that modern warfare now requires. In some ways, their peacetime tasks are indistinguishable from those of civilians in business or government. The senior commanders do not come from these ranks; they tend to be conservative—in the sense that they set great store by tradition and the old virtues—and they ultimately set the tone for all.

By British or German standards, the American military culture is highly informal, especially in the Air Force and Army. These services, in peacetime, tend to reflect, to a considerable degree, the manners and mores of the larger society. In a real sense, the military since World War II has served as the vanguard of social change, notably with respect to racial integration. (Not surprisingly, the partial integration of women has proved, in many ways, far more difficult.) Discipline is less than harsh. Even so, the bottom line remains and is constantly invoked: duty, honor, country.

As in the past, few military commanders are zealots on economic matters, except as they worry about the radical ups and downs (reflecting national moods) in defense spending. They obey their civilian superiors, although with some resentment over the politicians' chronic quest for short-term political gain; the Vietnam veterans remember with some bitterness that they were dispatched by politicians to fight a war they were not allowed to win. After long experience with men in uniform, they take a skeptical view of the practicality of generalized social uplift. Now, as in the past, they worry about the public's readiness to sacrifice for the nation, the stress on consumerism, self-interest, hedonism—on rights as opposed to duties. Not surprisingly, given the media's focus on conflict, deviance, and melodrama, most senior military men do not see the media as allies of civic peace and virtue.

The senior military officers are no longer primarily drawn, as they were prior to World War II, from the southern gentry or the northern upper-middle class. The typical officers' club smacks more of the Holiday Inn than of the Chevy Chase Club, and the sheer size of the officer corps makes it unlikely that the small, self-contained service community that prevailed prior to World War II will reemerge.

Robert Lichter and Stanley Rothman have surveyed attitudes, social origins, and voting habits of the "military elite." In general, they find no less a gap between senior military officers and those in the media than between businessmen and journalists, but on some topics businessmen and the military do not see eye to eye either (a finding that reaffirms the conclusions of Janowitz 30 years ago). In general, the military remain conservative on social values, responsive to political candidates who favor higher defense spending, and far less apt than media people to see the United States and the West as the source of the Third World's problems. According to Lichter and Rothman, the social values of senior officers are closer to those of Middle America than to those of the more permissive members of the media on such matters as adultery, homosexuality, and abortion.

The senior officers are from Middle America mostly, and, academy graduates aside, they did not attend elite colleges. On the other hand, they keep going to school. The Army, in particular, encourages graduate education. Peacetime service abroad brings a certain worldly sophistication; and the senior generals and admirals are no strangers to political Washington or to diplomatic life.

In peacetime, senior military officers are, in fact, deeply involved in bureaucratic politics. Troops and equipment must be kept in as high a state of readiness as possible despite the distractions of peacetime. But in Washington, each service chief is preoccupied with maintaining or enlarging budget share, devising strategic rationales for his service's programs, and adjudicating competing intraservice claims for budget priority (e.g., aircraft carriers versus nuclear submarines in the Navy). He and his staff, therefore, must pay heed to the mood of Congress, the predilections of the White House and the Secretary of Defense, and stories in the press and television that may affect the service's image. Not surprisingly, the negative stories (scandal, misdeeds, mismanagement, waste) not only loom largest in the minds of Washington newsmen (they are more exciting to read) but also in the memories of the senior military (accurate or not, such stories may damage a man's career). Such stories may be exploited by rival services or by critics of the military on Capitol Hill, and they always tend to cause distress within the Pentagon.

The news media, like the armed services, have their various branches—wire services, newspapers, news magazines, radio, television—each with its own incentives and practices. Journalists also have developed a public theology: the press seeks out the facts, acts as watchdog over government, provides the truth so that serious citizens may decide; it may even serve as a kind of fourth branch of government. The First Amendment assures journalists the right to publish and is interpreted by some journalists as encompassing the right to gather news. But there is no counterpart in journalism to "duty, honor, country," or to the military leader's ultimate responsibility for life and death.

In peacetime, a free and vigorous press keeps democracy vigorous. Yet, as the military will point out, a democracy in wartime can survive without a First Amendment (indeed, press freedom is usually curbed), but it cannot survive without a successful military defense.

During the Cold War, the ambiguities of national security led to recurrent debate over the press's rights and responsibilities—a debate that intensified during the Vietnam conflict, when White House credibility was at an unusually and increasingly low ebb, and revived after the 1983 Grenada invasion.

Coexisting with journalism's public theology is an underlying reality: the news organizations are relatively small, competing commercial enterprises, operating under economic constraints, heavily dependent on attracting and retaining sufficiently large audiences to draw advertising and thus revenue. If reporters often write for each other, their superiors have the audience in mind; and they shape the news at least in part with an eye toward the average reader's or viewer's presumed interests or tastes.

Producing a network evening news show (or even a small segment of it) requires a high degree of coordination, supervision, editing skill, processing, and sizable numbers of support personnel. As NBC's Douglas Kiker once said, television newsmen are engaged in "making little movies." News magazine stories are products of group journalism: field reporters (often dispersed); researchers; rewritemen; editors. Wire services, through the editing and rewriting process, may blend the work of several field reporters. Newspapers, however, rely most heavily on the individual reporter in the field; his story may be shortened or dropped entirely, but under the rules of the craft it is seldom totally rewritten. It is the newspaper, oldest of the media, that provides the essentials of journalism's public theology, and it is here that the watchdog function is most highly rewarded in terms of professional esteem.

It is often said by newspapermen that they provide the first rough draft of history. But it is a very rough draft, for journalists are not political scientists, military analysts, intelligence officers, or foreign policy historians. News is not simply information. *The Washington Post* is not the *World Almanac* (or even, say, the *Congressional Quarterly*). Newsmen are both fact-gatherers and storytellers—

their product is not called a "report" or a "study." It is called a "story." And much news consists simply of good stories, dramas with human appeal. Every news organization's idea of a good story is just a little bit different. Warehouse fires, airplane crashes, murder trials, train wrecks are always good stories: they are diverting incidents. News, depending on the standards of the producing organization, is in part an art form. The conventions are learned on the job.

As Roger Rosenblatt pointed out in *Time:*

> Journalism tends to focus on the poor [for example] when the poor make news, usually dramatic news like a tenement fire or a march on Washington. But the poor are poor all the time. It is not journalism's ordinary business to deal with the unstartling normalities of life. Reporters need a *story,* something shapely and elegant. Poverty is disorderly, anticlimactic, and endless. . . . Journalism inevitably imposes forms of order on both the facts in a story and on the arrangement of stories itself. The structures of magazines and newspapers impose one kind of order, radio and television another, usually sequential. But every form journalism takes is designed to draw the public's attention to what the editors deem most important in a day's or week's events. This naturally violates the larger truth of a chaotic universe.

What kind of people are journalists? Like military life, the life of the journalist appeals to certain personality types. But recruits to journalism are usually very different from those who join the military. Reporters—however pressed by deadlines, by the tastes of superiors, by constraints of space and time, by the search for fresh information—are not *doers,* but observers. Reporters have no rank. Their status depends in large measure on their affiliation with (and within) a news organization ("I'm Joe Smith of *The New York Times*). They have little or no responsibility for other people. They are not team players, but competitive types within their own organizations, determined to keep up with, or beat, other news organizations. They are aggressive—on occasion, they must, by telephone or in person, cajole reluctant people into divulging information. They must necessarily both confront and gain the confidence of people in authority. They are watchdogs, but in Washington by far the largest share of their work consists of transmitting official news (of the executive branch or of Congress) based on official sources and, when possible, giving both sides of the story.

These reporters and their bosses must deal with a variety of ever-changing "realities"; in order to retain sanity, they must reduce complexity to a changing set of clichés. They have little time, or temperament, for reflection on the national interest or the Big Picture; they must operate on professional instincts; their memories are overwhelmed by the daily rush of new experiences, new faces, new facts—indeed, they prize such novelty. As storytellers, they prefer stories of people to stories of organizations; they prefer politics to government; they prefer action or events to patterns or trends. They like to be in the know; they are quickly bored or frustrated when there is no news, no new turn of events. Yet, they hate to be taken unawares; big surprises are unpleasant. Surprises may require a journalist to assimilate a new set of facts instantly and then to explain them under a tight deadline, which often means discarding acquired wisdom; it is no wonder that journalists tend to overreact, like Wall Street, to surprise, and tend to magnify any sudden crisis.

Almost as if in compensation for these professional strains, even big-league reporters are permitted a certain latitude in dress, behavior, off-duty life. The image of the cynical, hard-drinking reporter of *The Front Page* may have evolved to that of the well-paid (if not always well-read) liberal arts graduate, male or female, who writes news analysis as well as straight news. But a certain tolerance and rumpled informality still characterize the craft. Getting an important fact wrong, by omission or commission, prompts more frowns from the editors than it once did, but, unless libel is involved, it seldom leads to dismissal. Of late, errors may lead to published corrections. But editors do not like to discourage reporters unduly from the pursuit of good stories. On most newspapers, the reporter who does not *produce* many good page-one stories is in more trouble than the reporter who produces such stories that may, occasionally, be a bit one-sided, unduly alarmist, or biased.

The radical newcomer is, of course, television news, whose demands on correspondents are far more exacting. Television news is the offspring of Hollywood, the newsreels, and radio broadcasting; as ABC Producer Av Westin once put it, television news is just another branch of television. It is a different art form, only thinly related to print. If the print media have a fondness for the emotive human interest story as a side dish to hard news, television actually lives by it. No print journalist on a major newspaper or wire service would be permitted the latitude allowed television reporters as they interpret on-camera the carefully edited film snippets that appear on the network evening news shows. The television cameras cannot show a battlefield or an election; they can show men jumping off a helicopter or a voter at the polls. Indeed, the vignette, often presented by the correspondent as a microcosm of the larger event, is the goal of television news. The important thing for the television correspondent is to be there with his camera crew—at the firefight, at the warehouse fire, at the protest demonstration, at the *spectacle*—and get a filmed bit of drama with his brief narration to New York in time for the evening news. Unlike the print journalist, the television reporter cannot recoup. Either his cameraman has good film or he does not. To the television reporter, the fact-gathering, the map briefings, and information are secondary; in a 50-word script, he cannot use much information anyway; and what the home office wants him to do, essentially, is direct the making of a vivid little action film, and supply theme and coherence to the pictures with his script. As Michael Arlen has noted, what is important is not just the reality of the filmed event, but what the audience can be made to *feel* about it.

The reporter works for a television network whose existence is mapped by audience ratings; his superiors are well paid but suffer from chronic turnover. Like an actor, the TV reporter has an agent to represent him in negotiations with his employer. He is a name, a face. His world is vastly different from that of his faceless print colleagues.

Are journalists' biases political? Much has been written since Vietnam and Watergate about bias in the news. And there is no question that when they step into the voting booths, journalists tend to vote Democratic. Lichter and Rothman interviewed 240 journalists and broadcasters working for the big-league news media. They did not separate the differences in views of reporters and supervisors, those in broadcast or print news. But their findings would at first glance suggest that the charges of liberal bias were well founded. For example, during the four presidential elections from 1964 to 1976, an average of 86 percent of their respondents voted for the Democratic candidate. On some issues, notably abortion, affirmative action, environmental protection, they strongly favored the liberal side. Fifty-four percent of them described themselves as "liberals" or "left of center," while only 19 percent described themselves as "conservatives."

Yet, as other analysts point out, one must examine more closely how deeply held these personal views are, and how important they are in the selection and treatment of news stories on given topics. For example, in a widely quoted interview with *Variety*, Walter Cronkite defined himself as a liberal, and defined liberal as "one who is not bound by doctrine or committed to a point of view in advance." Herbert J. Gans said that the liberalism of journalists is a synonym for being "independent, open-minded, or both." Michael Robinson suggests that the television networks in particular seem to be, in the final product, "cynical, yes, but liberal, no . . . over the long haul, the national press is biased against everybody [in authority] but in near equal proportions."

Both Gans and Austin Ranney suggest that for television in particular, the ideological bias is not partisan, in the sense of being Republican or Democratic. It is a legacy of the Progressive movement at the turn of the century, when muckraking journalists like Lincoln Steffens maintained that the journalist's prime purpose was to uncover the wrongdoing and chicanery of big-city politicians, the robber barons, and other villains in positions of power. Such exposure of abuses would encourage serious citizens to band together to throw out the rascals, to change things, to put enlightened reformers in office. This spirit fits in with journalism's theology. Indeed, newspapermen have always cherished exposés of individual official wrongdoing, particularly those which prompt remedial or punitive action by prosecutors or legislative committees. Such exposés are good stories. They win Pulitzer prizes for their authors. They satisfy journalism's claim under the First Amendment to social utility beyond the simple transmission of news or entertainment.

From Progressivism comes the self-image of the press as the watchdog of all in authority, military or political. It is a self-image that may wax, as during the Watergate era, and wane, as it has of late. But it leads to good stories, particularly television stories, of individuals against authority (enlisted men against the brass), of dissident movements, of victims of war, corporate greed or poverty—stories which have intrinsic appeal. In matters of crime, for example, the press likes crime waves (real or imagined), but through the neo-Progressive 1970s, the plight of convicted murderers, rapists, and muggers locked up in prisons ("prison reform") got far more attention than the plight of their victims. This was not simply a question of populism; it was also a reflection of the fact that investigating reporters could see the prisons, the system, and the unhappy prisoners as an all-of-a-piece story; they could not see the victims in a single dramatic setting.

Overall, then, the biases of the press, and particularly television, are professional biases; for example, the incident that—by implication at least—can be presented as a microcosm, a symbolic story (e.g., the Zippo-burning of Cam Ne hamlet in Vietnam), or exposed as a cover-up (e.g., the Pentagon's failure to announce the bombing of the [unmarked] mental hospital on Grenada or excessive use of firepower in Panama). Again, especially in television, newsmen like people stories rather than complicated policy or organization stories.

The anti-authority biases do not manifest themselves in an all-pervasive manner. Journalists are dependent on their news sources, whether presidents or generals, and the president gets his say. Most news is "official news." But if any authority figure is found consistently to contradict himself, manipulate the facts, or shave the truth, the journalists will dutifully report what he (or she) has said; but they will begin to grumble among themselves, to nitpick his statements, and to quote more of his critics. When Big Bad Events catch him, they will not give him the benefit of the doubt, and his entire regime will suffer as well. Such was the fate of Lyndon Johnson over Tet in 1968 and Richard Nixon over Watergate in 1973–74. To this day, however, there are military men (and others) who blame it all on the media's liberal bias.

They cannot explain the difficulties of Jimmy Carter . . . or the success of Ronald Reagan, who, according to his aide Michael Deaver, "enjoyed a fair press," despite the lack of ideological sympathy among White House reporters. Why is this? The populism of the news media is selective. Newsmen respond to officials who are not afraid of them. Most of all, they respect winners (and pick on losers). They heed the presidential popularity polls. In most cases, they respond to candor, friendliness, and coherence, and distrust excessive sales-manship.

General Creighton W. Abrams, for example, enjoyed a generally favorable press during his difficult 1968–73 tour as U.S. commander in Vietnam. He regarded the press as a necessary evil. He did not attempt to sell administration policy. He sent newsmen with his troops into Cambodia in 1970. He met with individual senior newsmen in Saigon but otherwise kept a low profile. He held no press conferences, unlike his predecessor General William C. Westmore-land, who, deferring to Lyndon Johnson's wishes, twice came home to Washington to shore up public support for a war policy with which, on major strategic issues, he privately disagreed. In media retrospectives on the war, Westmoreland has suffered for that high visibility ever since.

The military culture, with its accent on conformity, control, discipline, accountability, group loyalty, and cohesion, finds itself in wartime up against a group that is individualistic, competitive, word-conscious, impatient, lacking for the most part internal rules or standards, varied in its needs, suspicious of authority, and hard-pressed by deadlines and the need to obtain good film or adequate information on short notice to satisfy the home office. However, as experience in Vietnam, Korea, and World War II made clear, the two cultures can work together when the military sets out consistent ground rules and is able to enforce them impartially and with some intelligence.

Essentially, as several of the essays in this volume tend to suggest, each side must go beyond the irritations and anxieties of the moment. Both Richard Halloran and Bernard Trainor usefully point out the necessity for the military never to forget that the press and television play an important role in maintaining the health of American democracy. As Halloran further notes, those journalists who abuse their prerogatives need not be given the same access or assistance rendered to their more competent brethren. All newspeople are not alike; all are not, as one Army wag in Riyadh put it, "Yuppies in the desert."

Military men should also understand that ultimately public support for American interventions overseas will depend less on media manipulation or the changing moods of journalists than on the words and deeds of the man in the White House—and progress on the battlefield. The lesson of Vietnam, as William Hammond points out in the present volume, is not that the press and television turned the citizenry against the war effort, but rather that Lyndon Johnson substituted public relations for a decisive strategy and thereby, as U.S. losses grew, slowly demoralized and divided the country, including the Congress and the press. We should also note among the essays in this book William Rusher's bleak scenario for the future. What it means to me is this: in committing U.S. forces to a prolonged military operation, the President must lead—and leadership may require a declaration of war or its equivalent.

Thus, in late 20th-century America, the military-media relationship, traditionally thorny, reflects the larger relationship between the government and the American people. And in wartime, for America to succeed, that relationship must be one of mutual trust and comprehension.

Peter Braestrup

.... 1

The Army and Public Affairs: A Glance Back ...

By William M. Hammond

Revolutionary War soldier and patriot Joel Barlow wrote shortly after the War for Independence that what separated free men from the oppressed was "a habit of thinking." Men submitted to a king, he said, not because that ruler was stronger or wiser than they but because of a belief that he was born to govern. In the same way, they became free when the conviction grew in them that they were in themselves equal to one another. The idea alone was what counted: "Let the people have time to become thoroughly and soberly grounded in the doctrine of equality, and there is no danger of oppression either from government or from anarchy." It was the American people's habit of thinking "that all men are equal in their rights," Barlow avowed, that had compelled them to revolt from Great Britain and that sustained their independence.[1]

Historians might quibble with Barlow's further conclusion that men will always act in their own best interests if only shown where those interests lie, but his insight into the American character and the nature of the American political experiment was important. For the founders of the United States had indeed constructed not just a new form of government but a new conception of politics: one rooted in the habit of equality and expressed by the principle that, as Charles Pinckney of South Carolina put it, "all authority flows from and returns at stated periods to, the people."² Yet, if that concept has been "the pivot," as James Madison observed, upon which the entire American system has revolved,³ it has also been a source of complication for the United States Army. For although the American soldier has taken pride in his role as guardian of the republic, he has also had to contend in time of war with the inefficiencies imposed by his nation's unique egalitarian and democratic psychology. Individual commanders have responded to that challenge differently, some more adequately than others. To all of them, however, good public relations—toward the people, who supply the troops; the Congress, which provides the money; the troops, who do the fighting; and the news media, which *The Federalist Papers* regarded as the "expeditious messenger" that would help concerned citizens "sound the alarm" should government become involved in "any pernicious project"⁴—have been of vital importance.

George Washington understood the nature of the American point of view. A member of the militia rather than a professional soldier, he understood that the men who followed him were themselves civilian in attitude and that European methods of command would never work in the American environment. As the great organizer of the Continental Army, Baron Friedrich Wilhelm von Steuben, put it in a letter to Benjamin Franklin, the American soldier was different from his European counterpart. Both were good fighters, but the European would obey an order without question while the American demanded an explanation. Washington thus put aside the threats of flogging and execution that constituted a large part of the British army's system of discipline and appealed instead to his soldiers' intelligence and their sense of loyalty to their communities. The attitude that permeated his command was summarized in the *Regulations for the Order and Discipline of the Troops of the United States* (better known as "The Blue Book") published in 1779: A captain's "first object should be to gain the love of his men, by treating them with every possible kindness and humanity, enquiring into their complaints and when well founded, seeing them redressed. He should know every man of his company by name and character."⁵

Washington recognized that his army of civilians needed the support of the civilian community if it was to succeed. He thus kept up a running dialogue with Congress, appealing for assistance and supplies, but also did what he could to maintain the morale of the legislators' constituents at home. The approach that emerged was simple. Washington and his commanders made patriotic speeches where they could but relied mainly upon the organs of the civilian community— the churches, the press, the pronouncements of the various county and state governments—to carry their message. After a defeat, Washington invariably accepted and spread exaggerated reports of enemy casualties to keep the people from becoming discouraged, but he was also keenly aware that facts spoke louder than propaganda.⁶ When Congress recommended that he commandeer supplies at bayonet point for his starving troops at Valley Forge, he refused the suggestion. He understood that American soldiers would earn the gratitude of the people by suffering hardship, even as the British earned their hatred by plundering the countryside.[7]

Since the newspapers of America were heavily favorable to the revolution and enjoyed wide circulation (in 1778 the *Connecticut Courant* claimed an amazing 8000 readers), Washington made it a point to support them. He afforded patriot editors fleeing from the British the protection of his Army and on one occasion even supplied a publisher with valuable tenting cloth for the manufacture of paper so that the troops would have an opportunity to read a newspaper. The press responded by fanning the flames of revolution. Printers published eyewitness accounts of battles and official communiqués from Washington and other generals. They made the depravity of the British a prominent theme and called again and again for public support for the Army. The effect on the public is difficult to gauge from two hundred years' distance, but some of it can be seen in the letters to the editor that appeared in the newspapers of the day. Writers lavished attention on the Army, referring to its men as "the boys from home" and warning solicitously that parents would hold military leaders strictly accountable for the "moral conduct" of their sons, who should be protected from "gaming, profaneness, and debauchery."[8]

George Washington understood that the war he fought was in part a public opinion war. He wanted victories on the battlefield but refused to achieve them at the expense of the people he hoped to influence. History ruled in his favor. The surrender of Lord Cornwallis at Yorktown would have been only a momentary lapse for the British, but for the conviction of Britain's rulers that the people of America were united against them and that further struggle would be futile.

In the years that followed the American Revolution, the habit of mind of the American people remained much as it had been in Barlow's day, but the military tended to forget the lesson taught of Washington's example. Concentrating on the truth that in battle men must obey to survive and shunned by a civilian community that held standing armies in suspicion as a threat to civil liberties, the professional soldiers of the Army withdrew into their own community. Andrew Jackson exemplified the attitude of many soldiers during the War of 1812. Preparing the defenses of New Orleans, he put an end to rumors that local leaders were contemplating some sort of capitulation to the British by threatening to blow up their meeting place, the city hall. The people reciprocated. Feelings against Jackson ran so high in the city after the return of peace that the courts forced him to pay a $1000 fine for failing to obey a writ of habeas corpus.[9]

The Army suffered no broadly adverse public consequences from the general's actions at New Orleans because the city in 1814 was relatively isolated from the rest of the United States and Jackson was one of the few legitimate heroes the war had produced. Circumstances changed in the years that followed. The growth of literacy, the invention of the telegraph, and continuing developments in the technology of news-gathering drew the territories of the United States more and more closely together. By 1860, more than 50,000 miles of telegraph wire spanned the country, and newspapers were in daily, sometimes bitter competition for the latest word on anything of importance that happened anywhere. The public, for its part, fell in with the development and accepted it as a matter of course.

The change had profound implications for the Army when the Civil War began, because commanders had to harmonize their concern for military security with a news-reporting situation that required the utmost discretion. The newspapers, on the one hand, were of little mind to observe official restrictions and were clearly capable of informing the enemy of Union dispositions and developments in time to have an effect on the outcome of a battle. The war, on the other hand, was once again a conflict for public opinion in which the morale of the Congress, the American people, and the soldier was of vital importance. The public itself was dangerously divided on whether to continue the fight and hungry for news of what was happening in the field. In New York City alone the circulation of the newspapers could increase by five times when word of a major battle arrived.[10] The troops were just as news-hungry. When the war entered Pennsylvania, the *Philadelphia Inquirer* often sold up to 25,000 copies of a single issue to the men in the field.[11] During a lull in the Battle of Cedar Creek in October 1864, observers later remarked that the first thing the men did all along the line was to sit down, boil coffee, and pull out their newspapers.[12]

Neither the military nor the government of President Abraham Lincoln came to terms with the problem. The War Department imposed censorship immediately after the Battle of Bull Run, but the enterprise limped throughout the war, hampered by confusion over whether the State Department, the Treasury, or the War Department had jurisdiction. In a vain attempt to counteract the rumors and misinformation appearing in the press, the Secretary of War early in 1864 began to issue his own dispatches through the Associated Press. Yet if his effort had any effect it was small. Official communiqués lacked the color that creative newsmen working from the barest minimum of information could provide. President Lincoln suppressed a number of small and large newspapers across the country for security violations. Yet even that made little difference. The public demanded news and the press intended to supply it, whether it existed or not.[13]

The public affairs function in the field was likewise mainly a matter of improvisation. Each commander had his own policy for handling the press. Politically oriented generals cultivated reporters and even wrote articles for publication in the newspapers. The professionals, meanwhile, hated newsmen for the misinformation they spread and the damage they could do both to security and to the careers of commanders. General Sherman, in particular, questioned the government's practice of allowing newsmen to accompany the armies. The accounts of battle appearing in the press were to him "false, false as hell," and the readers of such drivel little more than an unthinking herd.

"Vox populi?" he questioned; "Vox humbug!" As a result, one *New York Tribune* correspondent complained, "A cat in hell without claws is nothing [compared] to a reporter in General Sherman's army."[14]

Grant was bitter as well, but in better touch with the realities facing the government. He recognized that a significant number of Americans disagreed with the war and that President Lincoln was experiencing grave political problems because of the war's lack of progress. Prior to the great victories of 1864 at Atlanta and in the Shenandoah Valley, he said, war weariness became so pronounced that "anything that could have prolonged the war a year beyond the time when it did finally close would probably have exhausted the North to such an extent that they might have abandoned the contest and agreed to a separation." Grant believed that the Northern press was worth more than 100,000 fighting men to Lee and envied the supposed ability of the Confederate government to control its news media. Yet he recognized that good public affairs dictated a more lenient policy, if only to maintain the government's communications with the American people. "In the North," he observed, echoing Pinckney and Madison, "the people governed and could stop hostilities whenever they chose to stop supplies."[15]

For his own part, while criticized brutally at times by the press, Grant had the good sense to cultivate relations with at least one prominent reporter, Sylvanus Cadwallder of the *New York Tribune*. The newsman accompanied Grant on most of the general's campaigns and was even present at Appomattox Courthouse on the day Lee surrendered. So trusted was he that on one occasion he made a dangerous ride through enemy lines with a private message from Grant to Lincoln informing the President that the general intended to prevail in the Wilderness even if the effort took all summer. The reports that originated from Grant's relationship with Cadwallder, as a result, were relatively straightforward. In contrast to the word that came from Sherman's army, they certainly helped to quiet public concern that the war would go on without end.[16]

In the years following the Civil War, American suspicion of the military continued. Congress, as in the past, kept the Army carefully subordinate to civilian authority and spent little more than necessary to subdue the Indians and secure the continent. In 1877 it even failed to pass the military appropriation bill, forcing officers to go into debt to continue in the service. Although there was obviously a compelling need for the sort of public and congressional understanding that would pave the way for a substantial standing force, none materialized. Safe behind their ocean moats, Americans continued to put their greatest reliance on the militia in case of emergency and to arm in haste only when war seemed imminent.

The military, for its part, nursed wounds left over from the Civil War. Although a newsman died with General Custer at the Battle of the Little Big Horn, reporters accompanying military expeditions continued to be at best a nuisance as far as most officers were concerned. The commander of the

American expeditionary force to Cuba during the Spanish American War, General William R. Shafter, summarized the military's attitude. Unprepared for a request from the famous war correspondent Richard Harding Davis to go ashore with the first wave of troops at Daiquiri and intent upon the business at hand, he swore angrily at the reporter: "I don't give a damn who you are. I'll treat you all alike!" Davis and other reporters reciprocated by vilifying Shafter.[17]

But the Spanish American War would have been a public relations disaster for the Army even if Shafter had exercised the utmost tact. The United States went into it unprepared and won, as Davis observed, because it had "euchred God's almighty storm and bluffed the eternal sea."[18] The press, in the event, was bound to see what was wrong and to report it.

In the years that followed, as the country once again subsided into peacetime complacency, the Army began at last to grapple seriously with the public relations prerequisites for achieving a higher level of defense preparedness. The potentially hostile navies of Britain and Germany roamed the seas to the east; Mexico, to the south, seemed continually absorbed by revolutions that threatened to boil over into American territory; and Japan to the west gave every appearance of becoming both commercial rival and military adversary.

The possibility of a conflict with Japan in 1907 served as the immediate catalyst for change. Nothing came of the threat, but the Chief of Staff of the Army, Major General James Franklin Bell, recognized that if a war had occurred the United States would again have been unprepared. He drafted a long-range plan of expansion and improvement to remedy the situation but perceived immediately that Congress would never go along without considerable persuasion. To that end, he established a board of distinguished citizens to conduct an investigation and recommend appropriate changes. On the side, he hired a retired Army officer, Major John A. Dapray, to handle public relations on the issue and appointed Captain (later Major General) Johnson Hagood to serve as a full-time liaison with Congress.[19]

Bell was forced to step aside when his vehicle struck a Washington trolley in one of the nation's first automobile accidents, but his successors took up the program and continued to press for military reforms. They achieved some successes but never completely overcame the reluctance of either Congress or the president to fund a larger Army. Only in December 1915, with World War I raging in Europe, did President Woodrow Wilson finally send a bill on national defense to Congress.

In the spring of 1916, with 5000 American troops operating in Mexico in search of Pancho Villa and preparations for possible involvement in Europe at last beginning, the Secretary of the Army, Newton Baker, appointed a personable young officer, Major Douglas MacArthur, to deal with the newspapermen who had begun to cover the activities at the War Department. Issuing news releases and granting interviews, MacArthur became the Army's first true public affairs officer.[20] Historian R. Ernest Dupuy maintains that it was largely through MacArthur's strenuous efforts that the military services overcame the American public's reluctance to accept the Selective Service Act of 1917.[21]

As part of the general effort to improve the Army's readiness, proposals had surfaced in military journals as early as 1907 seeking legislation to regulate the press in time of war.[22] In 1913, a one-time Spanish American War correspondent who admitted contritely to having committed dangerous security indiscretions himself, J. C. O'Laughlin, lectured at both the Army and Naval War Colleges on the advisability of some form of regulation. Two years later the Army War College itself published a book on relations between the Army and the press in wartime that proposed a system of control.[23]

Whatever the influence of those preparations, when the United States entered World War I, war reporting fell in with the patterns of propaganda already prevalent in Europe. President Woodrow Wilson reasoned, as had European leaders, that the outcome of the war depended powerfully on the people's will to sacrifice and persist. Over one million men had been casualties in the Battle of the Somme alone. On that account, Wilson established a Committee on Public Information under journalist George Creel to do everything it could to strengthen national determination. Evolving into a mammoth propaganda organization, the Creel Committee, as it was called, came to maintain offices in every neutral and Allied country. It issued a daily newspaper, operated a press service that fed information to the news media, produced films and foreign language publications, and enlisted a corps of 75,000 patriotic speakers reaching into every part of the nation. Its organs stressed the supposed barbarity of the German armies and the justice of the Allied cause. Wilson himself contributed forcefully to the effort by appealing in his speeches to American idealism. The war thus became in the eyes of many Americans an effort to end all wars and a crusade to make the world safe for democracy.[24]

The U.S. Army in France made fewer mistakes than it had during the Civil War and in Cuba but failed to rise above the Wilson Administration's tendency to propagandize and its own continuing suspicion of the press. Recognizing at last that the American soldier yearned for news of what was going on, for example, it provided him with his own newspaper, *Stars and Stripes*, authored by service personnel at military expense. The publication contributed greatly to Army morale, but its content nevertheless merged with the distorted themes appearing in the United States. In the same way, the Army's policies for handling war correspondents were cautious in the extreme. American newsmen who wished to report the war had to be accredited by a lengthy process that included a personal appearance before the Secretary of War, an oath to write the truth, and submission of a $10,000 bond to insure their proper conduct in the field. In France, they submitted their writing to military censors who operated under the intelligence directorate (G-2), the arm of the Army most certain to protect even the least significant military secrets.

Military men also tended to remain aloof from the press. The Commander of American forces, General John J. Pershing, for one, rarely gave interviews. When Westbrook Pegler of the United Press attempted to speak with the general, for example, he was ordered abruptly to "get the hell out of my office!" Even so, responding to the American public's continuing demand for as much news as possible from the front, the Army allowed American reporters considerable freedom to accompany the troops in the field. A number thus took up station with the units of their choice and returned to headquarters only long enough to have their reports censored and dispatched.

As for the censorship itself, the record is mixed. The Allies prided themselves on their democratic principles and publicized the fact that the news their publics received was more plentiful and freer of restraints than that of the enemy. As a result, although the press remained unsatisfied, American censors allowed at least the general facts of the war and even some unpalatable news to pass. The stream of propaganda and official information flowing from the Creel Committee and military agencies nevertheless so eclipsed what the civilian press produced that it was bound to color and distort the public's understanding of the war.[25]

Reporters had little choice but to cooperate while the fighting continued. They contented themselves with writing the sort of morale-building human interest stories that their readers relished and the censors loved. Afterwards, they denounced the public affairs efforts of the U.S. government so roundly and in such sweeping terms that the word *propaganda* acquired a whole new series of unsavory connotations.[26] The chief American censor for the U.S. Army in Europe, newsman Frederick Palmer, expressed the feelings of most responsible critics. Referring years afterward to the "double life" he had led during the war, he stated his belief that he had served as "a public liar to keep up the spirit of the armies and peoples of our side."[27] Other commentators were equally emphatic. If censorship had been necessary to defeat the Germans, they said, the military had exercised it stupidly and with unreasonable severity. The overenthusiastic idealism of civilian officials had meanwhile tricked both the press and the common man into believing the "foolish dream" that an Allied victory would usher in a new era of peace for mankind.[28]

Whatever the validity of those claims, the military during World War I had clearly allowed Sherman's type of mentality to overwhelm that of Washington and Grant. Inexperienced in the art of public affairs, the Army in the field had failed to harmonize its unquestioned need for security with the American public's equally legitimate requirement for honest information about the war. Military managers such as Pershing were quick to brush the press aside, and their censors were overly concerned with protecting every aspect of the developing American involvement, to the detriment of public understanding. In the event, the war ended quickly enough to preclude the sort of devastating backlash that Grant had foreseen during the Civil War,[29] but the consequences were still severe. By feeding the instinct of the American public and Congress to withdraw once more behind the oceans and to cut military expenditures, the public affairs effort actually handicapped the military's ability during the 1930s to prepare adequately for the coming of World War II.

The military nevertheless learned from the experience. Following the war, the Army's press relations section became the central coordinator of all activities that informed the public about the Army's functions, objectives, and problems. By 1930, each technical and administrative branch of the Army and most major posts had public affairs officers in residence. They prepared speeches for general officers, maintained liaison with the press, and insured that contacts with civilian organizations remained positive and helpful to the Army's goals. While those efforts were developing, the Army also attempted to inspire its personnel to improve relations with the general public. For example, as Chief of Staff, General Pershing strove to overcome his officers' continuing distaste for civilians by ordering his men to mingle with the people living in areas near military bases. The effort was only marginally successful. Pershing's directive was ahead of its time. Few officers complied.[30]

More productive was an attempt by the Public Affairs Branch during the 1930s to divorce itself from G-2. Reasoning that the intelligence directorate's exaggerated concern for secrecy hampered legitimate efforts to keep the public and Congress informed, information officers continually pressed for affiliation with an agency that represented a more flexible point of view. G-2 held on tenaciously but finally agreed on the eve of World War II to transfer the Public Affairs Branch to the Office of the Deputy Chief of Staff of the Army. As part of the arrangement, the agency maintained one observer in the public affairs section to assert security requirements but yielded final say on all disputed matters to higher authority.[31]

The coming of World War II served as a test of the military's increased sophistication with public affairs. Working from a recognition that neither the soldier nor the public would function well unless they had a keen appreciation of the importance of the war and of what was happening, the armed services attempted to keep both groups informed without releasing information of value to the enemy. The Army's Information and Education Division established radio stations to provide news and entertainment to the troops. *Stars and Stripes* reappeared. A magazine named *Yank* followed. A host of psychological and sociological studies undertook to learn how the soldier thought, what his fears were, and what would motivate him. They produced a fund of facts that aided leaders in determining how to deal with the troops' fear of German weapons, their attitudes toward being wounded, and how they felt about everything from food to pay.[32]

The ability of each nation involved to broadcast news electronically had a profound effect on the handling of the press during the war. Since it was clear that bad news would become public anyway, the United States and its allies attempted to keep both the troops and the public informed of at least general trends. Some correspondents complained that censorship was too stringent and that the Navy was particularly reluctant to release word of American losses—Admiral Ernest J. King, the Navy's chief, avowed that he would have preferred to release only one statement about the war, the one announcing victory—but the Army, for its part, succeeded in opening enough information to keep the press reasonably satisfied.

Conflicts between the security-conscious military and such civilian information agencies as the Office of War Information, which argued for the release of "everything known to the enemy or that would not give him aid," were nevertheless unavoidable.[33] As Secretary of War Henry L. Stimson complained, the problem of reconciling the two points of view was sometimes almost insurmountable. "I am," said Stimson, "in the position of the innocent bystander in the case of an attempt by a procession of the Ancient and Honorable Order of Hibernians and a procession of Orangemen to pass each other on the same street."[34] The military prevailed in disputes of that sort, and the results failed to justify the fears of many libertarians that greater official reticence would give "aid and comfort to men responsible for our military or civil failures." Although some commanders were hardly above overplaying their victories, battles during World War II were rarely misrepresented, and atrocity stories, fictional heroes, and outrageously inflated victories appeared less often than in World War I.[35]

This was due at least in part to the personalities and beliefs of the Army's commanders, especially the Chief of Staff, General George C. Marshall, and the Supreme Allied Commander in Europe, General Dwight D. Eisenhower. Marshall considered the individuality of the American soldier a priceless asset. He insisted on discipline and respect for leadership but demanded, as had Washington and Von Steuben, that commanders treat the soldier as a thinking human being. Marshall's attitude was clear in the instructions he gave for running *Stars and Stripes*. Although the newspaper's war stories were censored, there was to be no official control over anything else that appeared. The general understood that the policy would provoke some commanders, but he insisted that repression of any sort would destroy the paper's image "as the voice of the enlisted man."[36] "A soldier's newspaper, in these grave times, is more than a morale venture," he added. "It is a symbol of the things we are fighting to preserve and spread in this threatened world. It represents the free thought and free expression of a free people."[37]

If Marshall knew instinctively how to deal with the soldier, he had to learn how to deal with the press. At first he kept newsmen at a distance and delegated to his subordinates the task of explaining the Army's policies. Later, as he gained confidence, he held on-the-record briefings for important correspondents. By the time of the Normandy invasion, he was meeting with the press openly to appeal for understanding of the Army's problems and to argue in favor of commanders such as General George S. Patton, who were sometimes the subject of controversy.[38]

Through it all, he pressed his commanders to cultivate the press and he kept up a stream of suggestions to Army public affairs officers on ways to present the Army's story more effectively. Dictatorships had the advantage in marshalling men and materiel to battle, he told his associates, but well-informed democracies were stronger. Dictatorships fell to pieces completely when weakened leadership could no longer enforce conformity. But democracies, by virtue of the free participation by the people, were more resilient, tending to solidify in the face of adversity.[39]

Eisenhower shared Marshall's beliefs about the necessity for keeping the public informed. Convinced that democracies were incapable of waging war without widespread popular support, he asserted that Americans, in particular, "either will not or cannot fight at maximum efficiency unless they understand the why and wherefore of their orders."[40] Considering good relations with the press essential to the process of forging support at home and unity among America's allies in Europe, he made public affairs a command priority. Where General MacArthur in the Pacific kept reporters almost completely at bay, Eisenhower flattered newsmen by turning them into "quasi-members" of his staff. To build the reporters' trust, he also instructed his censors never to cut "personal criticism of me or of my actions" from press dispatches.[41] Reporters, as a result, developed great confidence in him. Although they occasionally criticized his decisions, they stood with him when it mattered. When he requested, for example, that they suppress for the sake of morale the story that General Patton had slapped an infirm soldier during the Sicilian campaign, they banned the news so completely that word of the incident took three months to reach newspapers in the United States.[42]

Relations with the press during World War II were so well maintained that few criticisms emerged when the conflict ended. True, writer Fletcher Pratt avowed that official censors had created a legend "that the war was won without a single mistake, by a command consisting exclusively of geniuses."[43] Novelist John Steinbeck alleged that the press cooperated so completely with the censors that it isolated the American public from the reality of the war.[44] And journalist Phillip Knightley suggested years later that the American public received little more news of the war than the people of Japan: what the government wanted known and nothing else.[45] The consensus of most commentators, however, has been that, under the circumstances and except in a few instances, World War II was accurately and honestly reported by both the government and the news media.[46]

The same could hardly be said for the wars that followed in Korea and Vietnam. At the start of the war in Korea, American commanders apparently expected the same sort of cooperation from the press that they had received during World War II. Lacking facilities to censor news dispatches, they imposed a system of voluntary guidelines for reporters to follow. The approach seemed successful at first. The United Nations Commander in Korea, General of the Army MacArthur, cabled the Department of the Army in September 1950 that he was reasonably satisfied. Free of censorship, he said, the press had afforded the American public almost complete coverage of the war, "without, as far as I know, a single security breach of a nature to provide effective assistance to the enemy."[47]

MacArthur changed his mind with the setbacks that accompanied Communist China's entry into the war. Hampered by fierce competition among reporters and by a failure to specify clearly what news was of value to the enemy, his system broke down. With breaches of security by the press almost a daily occurrence, he had little choice but to invoke censorship. The result was hardly satisfactory. Although the new rules succeeded in reducing the number of security violations, they failed to stop them completely. Those few reporters who were willing to flaunt their independence could still report freely when they traveled to Japan and the United States. As a result, on 18 June 1951, *Newsweek* published a map detailing the order of battle for the entire U.S. 8th Army.[48]

Military information officers, for their part, provoked the press on a number of occasions by extending censorship into areas of legitimate discussion and by withholding information on matters that had little to do with military security. When inmates rioted at a United Nations prisoner of war facility in April 1952, for example, the information officers withheld all word of the event lest it become an issue in armistice negotiations. They also delayed before releasing information on the seizure of the American commander of the Kojo-do POW camp by enemy inmates during May 1952. In both cases, word surfaced in the form of newspaper exposés that did more damage to the Army than to the negotiations.[49]

Although the Army's experience with public affairs during the Korean War was laden with problems,[50] the American news media appear for the most part to have supported the war. The same was true for the war in Vietnam, at least until the Tet Offensive in 1968. Prominent newspapers such as the *St. Louis Post Dispatch* and *The New York Times* consistently questioned U.S. policy in Southeast Asia, but most of the broadcast and print media supported President Lyndon Johnson's desire to keep communism from spreading in South Vietnam. If they disagreed at all it was with the tactics the United States chose to employ. Both they and their reporters in the field tended to believe that Americans should take charge of the war and carry it to a quick, clean conclusion.[51]

The public affairs policy adopted by the U.S. command in South Vietnam was built in part upon that fact. General William C. Westmoreland, in consultation with agencies in Washington, opted for a policy of voluntary guidelines for the press over censorship because he trusted the good will of the American correspondents reporting the war. Aware as well that the South Vietnamese would necessarily be a part of any censorship program that developed and that they were unsympathetic to the American idea of freedom of the press, he was also concerned that they might use censorship as a tool to intimidate reporters who criticized them. If that happened, it might alienate the American people, who had never shown much interest in the war but whose support, as in earlier conflicts, was all-important. Westmoreland supplemented his voluntary guidelines with a program that attempted to keep the press informed by providing regular background briefings for selected correspondents, 24-hour consultation services by knowledgeable public affairs officers, daily press conferences, transportation into the field for newsmen who wanted to see the war up close, and a system of press camps throughout Vietnam to supply reporters in the field with at least rudimentary amenities.

The effort had its effect, but in the end failed to compensate for major flaws in the American strategy. For by choosing to leave the enemy's sanctuaries in Laos and Cambodia intact and by refusing to invade North Vietnam or to block off the enemy's ports, the United States left the practical initiative to the communists. The foe chose when and where to fight. Under the circumstances, the only positive option left was to convince the enemy that there was no hope for his cause. Yet to do that, President Lyndon Johnson had first to win the support of a reluctant American public for a prolonged war of attrition by convincing it that South Vietnam was worth the effort and that American forces would win without a major sacrifice of lives and treasure.

But he could not bring it off. For many reasons—political immaturity brought on by years of French misrule, corruption, a lack of will brought on by exposure to the "take it over" attitude of the American military—the South Vietnamese were unreceptive to the sort of reforms that might have made their cause attractive to the American public. Furthermore, though U.S. forces seemed to win all the battles, the enemy never went away.

The Johnson Administration responded to the tensions that resulted by using all the facilities of the government and military services to mount public relations campaigns to demonstrate that the South Vietnamese armed forces were effective, that programs to win the hearts and minds of the country's peasantry were working, and that the American effort was indeed making progress. The news media replayed those themes, but each official statement of optimism seemed to have a pessimistic counterpart and each statistic showing progress an equally convincing opposite. Those ambiguities found their way into press sentiment as well, and into the nightly briefing for the Saigon correspondents, which soon became known to reporters and public affairs officers alike as "The Five O'Clock Follies."

As the war continued, public affairs officers found themselves caught between the President's efforts to shore up support for his policies and their own judgment that the military should remain above politics. They recommended that the public affairs apparatus in Vietnam deal only with military matters and leave to civilian agencies more suited to making political statements all attempts to justify the conflict. They were overruled by the Chairman of the Joint Chiefs of Staff, on grounds that the war required explanation in every way possible. As a result, by late 1967 members of the military were as involved in selling the war as the political appointees they served.

The effect of the policy could be seen in the evolving way the press viewed General Westmoreland. Prior to his trip to the United States in April 1967, when he addressed Congress and willingly joined President Johnson's attempts to market the war, his credibility with the press was high. Newsmen often replayed his background briefings in Saigon word for word in their reports. After he injected himself into the controversies surrounding the war, he became identified as a spokesman for the President's policies. From then on, his background briefings rarely appeared without comment. Reporters felt free to disagree with what he had to say.

Complicating the situation was a more general conflict in South Vietnam between the American press and military. Believing that the news media had generally supported official policy in earlier American wars, many members of the military expected similar support in Vietnam. When the failure of Johnson's strategy made that impossible, they blamed the press for the credibility problems they experienced. The news media, for their part, were hardly more forbearing. Citing a host of contradictions, reporters accused the military of attempting to mislead the American public. In the meantime, they misled the public themselves by sacrificing depth and analysis to color, while failing to make the most of the legitimate news within their reach. The good and bad points of the South Vietnamese army and government, the wars in Laos and Cambodia, the policies and objectives of the Hanoi regime and the Viet Cong, and even the M-16 rifle all probably received less coverage in the press, positive and negative, than they should have.

In the end, the war itself—rather than the press or the supposed failure of the government adequately to prepare the people for war—alienated the American public. Every time the number of Americans killed and wounded increased by a factor of ten—going from 1000 to 10,000, 10,000 to 100,000— public support as measured by the Gallup Poll fell 15 percentage points.[52] By 1972, public sentiment had turned decisively against the war. The fears Ulysses S. Grant had expressed during the American Civil War were echoed in a final message from Johnson's successor, President Richard Nixon, to the American Ambassador in South Vietnam, Ellsworth Bunker. The South Vietnamese, according to Nixon, would have to go along with the peace treaty the United States had concluded with North Vietnam "or we have to go it alone." The main defenders of the Administration's war policies in Congress, he said, had made it plain that if the objections of the Saigon regime posed the only roadblock to the agreement, they would themselves lead the fight to cut off all military and economic assistance to South Vietnam. Despite the mandate he had received in the 1972 presidential election, Nixon concluded, "The door has been slammed shut hard and fast by the long-time supporters of my policies in Vietnam in the House and Senate who control the purse strings. . . . The fat is on the fire. . . . It is time to fish or cut bait."[53]

The door Nixon referred to had swung back and forth repeatedly during American history, coming closer to shutting at some times than at others. George Washington had discerned its movement. So had Grant. The exaggerated hype that emerged from the effort to sell World War I was partly the result of an attempt to keep it open. The door caused few problems during

World War II, when the United States was under attack, but it is tempting to speculate about what would have happened if the Korean War had lasted much longer than it did. Recent analyses indicate that public support for that war declined in an inverse proportion to casualties by much the same degree as in Vietnam.[54]

If there is a lesson, or some enduring principle, to be drawn from the history of the Army's efforts at public affairs, it goes back to the statement by Joel Barlow, that Americans see themselves as equal in their rights and expect to be treated accordingly. Throughout much of its history, the Army has defended that precept but has found it difficult to reconcile with the requirement for secrecy that war imposes. During the 19th century the Army lacked a formal public affairs program and depended upon its officers and the central government to generate the support it needed. The result was often painful. For while some commanders were adept indeed at handling the people, their representatives in Congress, and the press, others such as Sherman were not. After every war, a period of decay usually set in. The Army survived, but often, it seemed, just barely.

During the 20th century, the Army undertook formal public affairs programs to compensate. They helped, but their success during World War II at the hands of such master communicators as Marshall and Eisenhower led to the growth of an idea that public relations could handle almost every problem. The concept flowered in Vietnam, where Johnson and his advisers appeared to gamble that public relations could win at home what they seemed unable to attain on the battlefield. Students of the well-placed leak, adept at manipulating both the electorate and the news media, they forgot at least two commonsense rules of effective advertising: first, that good public relations may indeed induce a buyer to purchase a product once, but all subsequent sales still depend on whether the product itself fulfills his expectations; second, that the truth has greater ultimate power than the most pleasing of bromides.

The Army clearly has both a right and an obligation to communicate its requirements to the American people and their representatives. To do otherwise would be to jeopardize its primary mission to defend the nation. Yet if history teaches anything, it advises commanders to maintain their credibility with the people at all times and to remain above the sort of political involvements that harmed Westmoreland's command. There are occasions when they must deal firmly with the nation's news media, but, for their own good if not out of principle, they must do so equitably and with a keen awareness that the concept of a free press emerged not from chance but out of the very fiber of the nation. Well-trained public affairs officers can help in this by becoming brokers who attempt to reconcile the military point of view with that of the civilian world. To do that, as one of the Army's greatest public affairs officers, Major General Winant Sidle, observed, those officers must be an integral part of the Army but must also cultivate a perspective that is somewhat apart. Only in that way can they serve the Army while doing their duty to the people.[55]

The American soldier, as Baron von Steuben observed, represents a unique point of view. It sometimes makes him difficult to deal with but it also makes him strong. In the same way, freedom of speech and of the press in time of war may sometimes be a problem, but they make the nation strong. In that, as a presidential commission on freedom of the press observed in 1947, they are similar to democracy itself—always in danger but always dangerous.[56]

Notes

1. Barlow is quoted by Gordon Wood, *The Creation of the American Republic* (Chapel Hill: Univ. of North Carolina Press for the Institute of Early American History and Culture, 1969), p. vii.

2. Charles Pinckney, quoted ibid., p. 596.

3. James Madison, "No. 63," *The Federalist* (New York: The Modern Library, 1937), p. 411.

4. See Alexander Hamilton, "No. 84," in *The Federalist Papers*, ed. Clinton Rossiter (New York: New American Library, 1961), p. 517.

5. *Regulations for the Order and Discipline of the Troops of the United States*, Part I, quoted in Robert K. Wright, *The Continental Army* (Washington: U.S. Army Center of Military History, 1983), p. 142.

6. James Thomas Flexner, *George Washington, The Forge of Experience* (Boston: Little, Brown, 1965), p. 255.

7. James Thomas Flexner, *Washington, The Indispensable Man* (Boston: Little, Brown, 1974), pp. 110–11.

8. Don Higginbotham, *The War of American Independence* (New York: Macmillan, 1971), pp. 258–63.

9. J. C. A. Stagg, *Mr. Madison's War: Politics, Diplomacy, and Warfare in the Early American Republic, 1783–1830* (New Jersey: Princeton Univ. Press, 1983), pp. 494–99.

10. Phillip Knightley, *The First Casualty* (New York: Harcourt, Brace, Jovanovich, 1975), p. 23.

11. Ibid., p. 27.

12. Interview with Mr. Kim Holein, Civil War historian, U.S. Army Center of Military History, 20 January 1988.

13. J. C. Andrews, *The North Reports the Civil War* (Pittsburgh: Univ. of Pittsburgh Press, 1955), p. 641. See also Knightley, p. 27.

14. Sherman is quoted in Joseph H. Ewing, "The New Sherman Letters," *American Heritage*, July 1987, pp. 24–41.

15. Ulysses S. Grant, quoted in John Formby, *The American Civil War* (New York: Charles Scribner's Sons, 1910), p. 327.

16. Knightley, p. 27.

17. E. J. McClernand, "The Santiago Campaign," in *The Santiago Campaign* (Richmond: Society of the Army of Santiago de Cuba, 1927), p. 10.

18. Richard Harding Davis, *The Cuban and Porto Rican Campaigns* (Freeport, N.Y.: Books for Libraries Press, 1970), p. 98.

19. This section is based upon an interview with Dr. Edgar Raines, Center of Military History historian and biographer of J. Franklin Bell, 15 January 1988.

20. D. Clayton James, *The Years of MacArthur* (Boston: Houghton Mifflin, 1970), I, 127–31.

21. Dupuy is quoted ibid., p. 131.

22. See, for example, Frank Geers, "The Government of War Correspondents," *Journal of the Military Service Institution*, 44 (May–June 1909), 416–17.

23. Joseph J. Mathews, *Reporting the Wars* (Minneapolis: Univ. of Minnesota Press, 1957), p. 209. See also U.S. War College Division, General Staff Corps, *The Proper Relation between the Army and the Press in War* (Washington: GPO, 1916).

24. William Hammond, "Propaganda: World War I and II," *The Dictionary of American History* (New York: Charles Scribner's Sons, 1978).

25. Mathews, pp. 171–72.

26. Ibid., pp. 155–58, 170–72, 175; Knightley, pp. 114–35; William M. Hammond, *The U.S. Army in Vietnam: The Military and the Media, 1962–1968* (Washington: U.S. Army Center of Military History, 1988), introduction.

27. Palmer is quoted in Mathews, p. 155.

28. Ibid., p. 157.

29. The same was not true for Germany. The case can be made that Kaiser Wilhelm's failure to inform his people of the reverses occurring on the Western Front left them unprepared for defeat and contributed materially to the confusion and chaos in the country's cities that followed the German army's surrender.

30. Addison F. McGhee and Kenneth L. Fox, "A History of the Office of the Chief of Information to include Its Missions and Functions," 11 September 1964, unpublished manuscript, Office of the Chief of Information, p. 18, copy in Center of Military History files.

31. Ibid., pp. 22–29.

32. F. H. Osborne, "Information and Education Division," *Military Review*, 24 (December 1944), 22–26.

33. Elmer Davis, Director, Office of War Information, quoted by John Morton Blum, *V Was for Victory: Politics and American Culture During World War II* (New York: Harcourt Brace Jovanovich, 1976), p. 34.

34. Henry L. Stimson, quoted ibid., p. 34.

35. Palmer Hoyt, Domestic Director, Office of War Information, "The Use and Abuse of Restraints," in *Journalism in Wartime, A Symposium of the School of Journalism, the University of Missouri*, ed. Frank Luther Mott (Washington: American Council on Public Affairs, 1943), pp. 42–43. See also Mathews, pp. 176, 214.

36. Mathews, p. 94.

37. George C. Marshall, quoted by Forrest C. Pogue, *George C. Marshall: Organizer of Victory, 1943–1945* (New York: Viking Press, 1973), p. 93.

38. Ibid., p. 359.

39. Ibid., p. 95.

40. E. K. G. Sixsmith, *Eisenhower as Military Commander* (New York: Stein and Day, 1973), p. 10. See also Steven E. Ambrose, *Eisenhower, 1890–1952* (New York: Simon and Schuster, 1983), p. 176.

41. Sixsmith, p. 71.

42. Ambrose, p. 176.

43. Fletcher Pratt, "How the Censors Rigged the News," *Harper's Magazine*, February 1946, p. 99.

44. John Steinbeck, *Once There Was a War* (London: Heinemann, 1959; Corgi Edition, 1961), pp. 11–15.

45. Knightley, pp. 301–2.

46. Mathews, p. 176.

47. Douglas MacArthur to the Department of the Army, quoted by D. Clayton James, *The Years of MacArthur* (Boston: Houghton Mifflin Company), III, 566.

48. B. C. Mossman, "Command and Press Relationships in the Korean Conflict," undated [1967] Center of Military History study, Center of Military History files.

49. Ibid.

50. See Knightley, pp. 336–56, for a brief, if highly opinionated, survey of public affairs problems during the war.

51. This section is based upon Hammond, *The U.S. Army in Vietnam: The Military and the Media, 1962–1968*, conclusion.

52. John Mueller, *War, Presidents, and Public Opinion* (New York: Wiley, 1973).

53. Message, Kissinger WHS 2257 to Bunker, 26 November 1972, repeating two memos from

Nixon to Kissinger. Quoted in Jeffrey Clarke, *The U.S. Army in Vietnam: Advice and Support, the Later Years* (Washington: U.S. Army Center of Military History, 1988), 491ff.

54. See Mueller.

55. Interview with Major General Winant Sidle, Chief of Information, U.S. Army, 12 July 1973.

56. See William Ernest Hocking, *Freedom of the Press, A Framework of Principle,* Report from the Commission on Freedom of the Press (Chicago: Univ. of Chicago Press, 1947).

This article appeared originally in the June 1989 issue of *Parameters* under the title "The Army and Public Affairs: Enduring Principles."

........2

The New
Sherman Letters ..

By Joseph H. Ewing

William Tecumseh Sherman, announced *The New York Times* near the end of the Civil War, "has surpassed all newspaper correspondents in writing about military affairs . . . for conciseness, perspicacity, and comprehensiveness with brevity he is the perfect model." One Associated Press reporter went so far as to say that the man would have been an even better war correspondent than a general.

But most newspapermen knew Sherman as a relentless enemy. As late as April 1865, a *New York Tribune* correspondent wrote that "a cat in hell without claws is nothing [compared] to a reporter in General Sherman's army."

From the First Battle of Bull Run to the end of the war, Sherman believed far more harm than good was done the Union cause by war correspondents. They were "dirty newspaper scribblers who have the impudence of Satan." They were "spies and defamers." They were "infamous lying dogs."

Hostility at this level pulses through a collection of 24 previously unpublished letters written by Sherman in the midst of the Civil War to my great-grandfather, Thomas Ewing, who was Sherman's foster father, and to my grandfather, Philemon B. Ewing, who was Sherman's boyhood companion. One of them, a 3000-word jeremiad, is the longest and most revealing discourse he ever composed on the subject.

This letter and its companions lay for 40 years or more in the bottom of a wooden box in my family's attic in Roselle, New Jersey, unseen by biographers or historians, although my father inventoried them and handled them with scholarly care. After his death I put the collection in a safe, where it remained generally undisturbed for another 30 years. If such benign neglect is considered an affront to the writing of history, I comfort myself with the thought that the letters at least have been preserved. . . .

After graduating from West Point, Sherman served in the Army for 13 years, his tour of duty taking him to Florida, South Carolina, California, Missouri, and Louisiana. In 1850 he married Ellen Boyle Ewing, one of Senator Ewing's daughters, who had grown up from childhood in the same house with him. Three years later he resigned his commission to enter upon successive careers in banking, law, business, and education. In his impressionable years at West Point, Sherman had absorbed much of the academy's aristocratic tradition and, in his close association with Southerners thereafter as both an officer and a civilian, he acquired a generally Southern outlook on life. Yet he remained a staunch Union man. In 1860 Sherman agreed to become the first superintendent of the newly established Louisiana State Seminary, but when Louisiana seceded in 1861, he departed for the North in deep distress. By July he was commanding a brigade of General Irvin McDowell's Army of the Potomac as it marched south toward Manassas, Virginia, for the first major clash of the war.

The cause of Sherman's enmity toward the press is simple: Northern newspapers repeatedly and in great detail alerted the South that an attack was imminent. The telegraph, the railroad, and the daily press had made it possible to disseminate information at a rate and in quantities undreamed of a generation before, but the newspapermen still saw their job in the old, simple terms: get out the story. That the story could now be gotten out with a speed that put its subjects' lives at hazard was not immediately apparent. Sherman was among the first—and was certainly the most vocal—of the military men who had to cope with the fact that the Industrial Revolution had overtaken the Bill of Rights. The dimensions of the problem became clear to him even before he went into battle.

On 17 July 1861, *The New York Times* reported: "The army in Virginia today took up the line of march for Richmond, via Fairfax and Manassas. The force starting today was fully fifty thousand strong . . . about three thousand Regular Infantry, Cavalry, and Artillery, and fifty thousand Volunteers. . . ." On the same day, the *Washington Star* provided a detailed order of battle: "The column on the extreme right is commanded by General Tyler. That consists of the following excellent troops, viz: the Maine Second, the First, Second, and Third Connecticut regiments; the New York Second, the First and Second Ohio. . . ."

The First Battle of Bull Run ended catastrophically for the North, and whether or not the newspapermen were to blame, the indiscretion of the press before the battle still burned in Sherman's mind two years later when he wrote his foster father: "Now in these modern times a class of men has been begotten & attend our camps & armies gathering minute information of our strength, plans & purposes & publishes them so as to reach the enemy in time to serve his purposes. Such publications do not add a man to our strength, in noways benefit us, but are invaluable to the enemy. You know that this class published in advance all the plans of the Manassas Movement [which] enabled [General Joseph E. Johnston] . . . to reinforce Beauregard whereby McDowell was defeated & the enemy gained tremendous strength & we lost in comparison. . . ."[1]

If Sherman had little patience with the press after Bull Run, however, the press soon would have no patience with him.

After his first fight, Sherman wrote of the "shameless flight of the armed mob we led into Virginia," and he expected to be discharged along with all the other leaders of the battle. But two weeks later the War Department announced the promotion of various colonels, "all of whom," Sherman wrote in his *Memoirs*, had "shared the common stampede." His name was among them. Now a brigadier general of volunteers, he was ordered west to Kentucky, to the newly formed Department of the Cumberland. . . .

When Kentucky, although a slave state, finally made up its official mind to remain in the Union, the Confederate general Albert Sidney Johnston advanced his Rebel troops into the state and began pushing toward Louisville. Against this invasion there was little at hand of organized military manpower, but Sherman was able to set out a defensive position using available home guards and volunteers. . . .

Many years after Sherman had become one of the nation's most experienced generals, he remained convinced that if Albert Sidney Johnston had pressed his advantage in 1861, "He could have walked into Louisville." All the while Northern newspapers continued to advertise the actual weakness of the Union position by revealing Sherman's operations. The *New York Tribune* on 17 October 1861 reported from Louisville that "Gen. Sherman now has at least twenty thousand men in the various camps between this city and Green River, and reinforcements arrive almost daily." There followed a list of recent reinforcements—"the Indiana 29th, 30th, and a remnant of the 6th . . . the Ohio 15th" and so on. When a copy of the paper came to Sherman's attention, he proclaimed that all reporters were henceforth banished from his lines.

Then, less than two weeks after taking over from Anderson, Sherman was paid an official visit by U.S. Secretary of War Simon Cameron, on his way back to Washington after a tour of the Western Department at St. Louis. With Cameron was Samuel Wilkerson of the *New York Tribune*, who was not identified as a reporter to Sherman and so was allowed to sit in on a discussion of the military situation in Kentucky. Sherman said he needed 60 thousand troops to drive the enemy from Kentucky, and 200 thousand to carry the war clear to the Gulf of Mexico. Apparently Secretary Cameron understood the 200 thousand figure as that deemed necessary for the defense of Kentucky. He considered the figure absurd but promised some additional men.

The official report of the Secretary of War's tour of Missouri and

Kentucky, which Wilkerson was believed to have had a large hand in writing, appeared in the *New York Tribune* on 30 October. This was not a leak. The report actually was released to the paper by Secretary Cameron, and there followed after the report an order of battle entitled *Exhibits No. 14,* explaining Union Army strength in Kentucky, which, incredibly, was carried by the *Tribune* in full.

As for Sherman personally, the report clearly insinuated that his mind was unstable and that he could not safely be entrusted with any important command. For some weeks, in fact, Sherman's officers and men had noticed that the general brooded day and night, that he lapsed into long silent moods, smoked incessantly, and paced up and down by the hour. It had begun to be whispered even before Secretary Cameron's visit that Sherman was suffering from depression. In any event, the 30 October report that appeared in the *New York Tribune* said specifically that on being asked what force he deemed necessary to defend Kentucky, Sherman "promptly replied 200,000 men. . . . The Secretary of War replied that . . . he thought Gen. Sherman over-estimated the number and power of the rebel forces; that the Government would furnish troops . . . but that he [the Secretary] was tired of defensive war . . . he begged Gen. Sherman to assume the offensive and to keep the rebels hereafter on the defensive. . . ."

It was clear that while Cameron was prepared to send additional troops to Kentucky, he was not about to entrust them to Sherman. A couple of weeks later General Don Carlos Buell was ordered to replace Sherman as commander of the Department of the Cumberland, an event greatly welcomed by the newspapermen there. The correspondent for the *Chicago Tribune* wrote that [Brigadier General Robert Anderson, the former commander of the Department of the Cumberland] "was a gentleman of no mind. Sherman is possessed of neither mind nor manners. We are thankful now that we have a man who combines both."

Sherman was ordered to inspect troops near St. Louis in the Department of the Missouri. Newspapers, however, kept alive the story that his mind was unbalanced, and Major General Henry W. Halleck, the department commander, placed him on a 20-day leave of absence, which Sherman spent in Lancaster, Ohio, with his wife and children. He was there when, on 11 December 1861, the *Cincinnati Commercial* announced some "painful intelligence": "Gen. William T. Sherman, late commander of the Department of the Cumberland, is insane. It appears that he was at the time while commanding in Kentucky, stark mad. . . . The harsh criticisms that have been lavished on this gentleman, provoked by his strange conduct, will now give way to feelings of deepest sympathy for him in his great calamity."

The story was picked up in papers across the country. Only time and success would dispel Sherman's mortification. After rumors circulated about Grant's drunkenness at the Battle of Shiloh, Sherman was able laughingly to attest to the friendship between them: "You see, Grant stood by me when I was crazy and I stood by him when he was drunk. . . ."

Late in July 1862 Sherman took over the District of Memphis, retaining command as well of his 5th Division, and that winter he led the first Union assault against Vicksburg—and thereby became embroiled, unintentionally, in a dramatic battle with Western war correspondents.

The massive Confederate battery at Vicksburg controlled the long southern sweep of the Mississippi from below Memphis to New Orleans. Sherman embarked his troops downriver on 19 December. Grant was to have taken part in the operation, but he withdrew at the outset when Rebel cavalry destroyed his supply base. Sherman went in alone and suffered 1700 casualties in a fruitless attempt to gain the Chickasaw Bluffs north of the city.

Ignoring Sherman's specific orders, an undetermined number of reporters had been aboard the Army transports. They now wrote their separate accounts of the disaster and mailed them to intermediaries in Memphis and Cairo, Illinois, for forwarding to their respective papers. However, Sherman's regional superintendent for the U.S. Army mails noticed these suspiciously fat envelopes and intercepted them. Not to be deterred, the correspondent for the *New York Herald*, Thomas W. Knox, angrily rewrote his account and then steamed upriver to Cairo, where he filed his dispatch without interference. In the *New York Herald* of Sunday, 18 January 1863, Knox's six-column story charged Sherman with gross, even criminal, negligence and confusion. "General Sherman was so exceedingly erratic," the story concluded, "that the discussion of a twelvemonth ago with respect to his sanity was revived with much earnestness. . . . Insanity and inefficiency have brought their result. Let us have them no more."

When Sherman saw the story, he immediately ordered Knox seized. He had the story read aloud to the reporter and demanded the source of each assertion. In a burst of honesty Knox declared, "Of course, General Sherman, I have no feeling against you personally, but you are regarded as the enemy of our set and we must in self-defense write you down." Sherman directed that papers be drawn up for Knox's court-martial.

On 6 February he wrote Senator Ewing about the press coverage of the Union defeat at Chickasaw Bluffs:

I am in battle & was pushed forward, catching all the path of the balls & bullets in front, and then the curses & malediction of the nonthinking herd behind. The Newspapers declare me their inveterate Enemy, and openly say they will write me down. In writing me down are they not writing the Cause and the Country down? Now I know and every officer knows that no army or detachment moves or can move that is not attended by correspondents of hundreds of newspapers. . . .

They encumber our transports, occupy state rooms to the exclusion of officers on duty, they eat our provisions, they swell the crowd of hangers on, and increase the impedimenta. They publish without stint positive information of movements past & prospective, organizations, names of commanders, and accurate information which reaches the enemy with as much regularity as it does our People. They write up one class of officers and down another, and fan the flames of discord and jealousy. Being in our very midst, catching expressions dropped by officers, clerks, and orderlies, and being keen expert men they detect movements and give notice of them. So that no matter how rapidly we move, our enemy has notice in advance. To them more than to any other cause do I trace the many failures that attend our army. While they cry about blood & slaughter they are the direct cause of more bloodshed than fifty times their number of armed Rebels. Never had an enemy a better corps of spies than our army carries along, paid, transported, and fed by the United States.

Then, less than two weeks later, with torrential rains hammering down on his camp, Sherman composed his fullest treatise on the villainy of the press in wartime. It is an eleven-page letter more vehement and more eloquent than any previously known statement by Sherman on the subject:

Camp Before Vicksburg, February 17, 1863

As I have more leisure than usual now I will illustrate by examples fresh in the memory of all, why I regard newspaper correspondents as spies & why as a servant of an enlightened government I feel bound in honor and in common honesty to shape my official conduct accordingly. A spy is one who furnishes an enemy with knowledge useful to him and dangerous to us. One who bears into a Fortress or Camp a baleful influence that encourages sedition or weakens us. He need not be an enemy, is often a trader woman or servant. Such characters are by all belligerents punished summarily with the extremist penalties, not because they are of themselves filled with guilty thought or intent but because he or she endangers the safety of an army, a nation, or the cause for which it is contending. [Major John] André carried no intelligence back to [English General Sir Henry] Clinton but was the mere instrument used to corrupt the fidelity of an officer holding an important command. Washington admitted the high and pure character of André but the safety of the cause demanded his punishment. It is hard to illustrate my point by reference to our past history, but I wish to convey the full idea that a nation & an army must defend its safety & existence by making acts militating against it criminal regardless of the mere interest of the instrument. We find a scout surveying our camp from a distance in noways threatening us but seeking information of the location, strength, and composition of our forces. We shoot him of course without asking a question. We find a stranger in our camp seeking a stray horse & find afterwards he has been to the enemy: We hang him as a spy because the safety of the army & the cause it fights for is too important to be risked by any pretext or chance. . . . I know the enemy received from the [press] . . . notice of our intended attack on Vicksburg & thwarted our well laid schemes. I know that Beauregard at Corinth received from the same source full details of all troops ascending the Tennessee and acted accordingly. I know that it was by absolute reticence only that Halleck succeeded in striking Forts Henry & Donaldson and prevented their reinforcement in time to thwart that most brilliant movement. And it was only by the absence of newspapers that we succeeded in reaching the post of Arkansas before it could be reinforced.

I *know* that the principal northern papers reach the enemy regularly & promptly & I know that all the viligance of our army cannot prevent it & I know that by this means the enemy can defeat us to the end of time. . . .

Another view of the case. The Northern Press either make public opinion or reflect it. By gradual steps public opinion instead of being governed governs our country. All bow to it & even military men who are sworn officers of the Executive Branch of the Government go behind & look to public opinion. The consequence is & has been that officers instead of keeping the Executive Branch advised of all movements, events, or circumstances that would enable it to act advisedly & with vigor communicate with the public direct through the Press so that the Government authorities are operated on by public opinion formed too often on false or interested information. This has weakened the Executive and has created jealousics, mistrust, & actual sedition. Officers find it easier to attain rank, renown, fame, and notoriety by the cheap process of newspapers. This cause has paralyzed several fine armies & by making the people at home mistrust the ability of Leaders, Surgeons, & Quarter Masters has even excited the fears of parents so far that many advise their sons and brothers to desert until desertion & mutiny have lost their odious character. I'll undertake to say that the army of the Potomac has not today for battle one half the men whom the U.S. pays as soldiers & this is partially the case with the army of the Tennessee & here.

In all armies there must be wide differences of opinion & partial causes of disaffection—want of pay, bad clothing, dismal camps, crowded transports, hospitals rudely formed, & all the incidents of war. These cannot be entirely avoided & newspapers can easily charge them to negligence of commanders & thereby create disaffection. I do not say the Press intends this but they have done this and are doing it all the time. Now I know I made the most minute and careful preparation for the sick & wounded on the Yazoo, plenty of ambulances & men detailed in advance to remove the wounded—four of the largest transports prepared & set aside before a shot was fired & that every wounded man was taken from the field dressed & carefully attended immediately & yet I know that the Press has succeeded in making the very reverse impression & that many good people think there was criminal negligence. The same naked representations were made at Shiloh & I saw hundreds of Physicians come down & when our Surgeons begged & implored their help they preferred to gather up trophies and consume the dainties provided for the wounded & go back and represent the cruelty of the Army Surgeons & boast of their own disinterested humanity. . . . Not a word of truth, not even a pretense of truth, but it is a popular & successful theme & they avail themselves of it. What is the consequence? All officers of industry who stand by at all times through storm & sunshine find their reputations blasted & others—usually the most lazy & indolent—reaping cheap glory & fame through the correspondents of the Press.

I say in giving intelligence to the enemy, in sowing discord & discontent in an army, these men fulfill all the conditions of spies. Shall we succumb or shall we meet and overcome the evil? I am satisfied they have cost the country hundreds of millions of dollars & brought our country to the brink of ruin & that unless the nuisance is abated we are lost.

Here we are in front of Vicksburg. The attack direct in front would in our frail transports be marked by the sinking of Steamers loaded with troops, a fearful assault against the hills fortified with great care by a cunning enemy. Every commander who has looked at it says it cannot be done in front—it must be turned. I tried it but newspaper correspondents had sent word in advance & ample preparations were made & [enemy] reinforcements double my number had reached Vicksburg. McClernand was unwilling to attack in front. Grant ditto. Then how turn the position? We cannot ascend the Yazoo to where our men can get a footing. We cannot run our frail transports past the Vicksburg Batteries, so we resolve to cut a channel into the Yazoo at the old pass near Delta above & into the Texas by way of Lake Providence. Secrecy & dispatch are the chief elements of success. The forces here are kept to occupy the attention of the enemy, two steamers are floated past the Batteries to control the River below & men are drawn secretly from Helena & Memphis to cut the canals & levees & remove all the inhabitants so that the enemy could not have notice till the floods of the Mississippi could finish the work of man. But what avail? Known spies accompany each expedition & we now read in the Northern papers . . . that our forces here are unequal to the direct assault but we are cutting the two canals above. The levees are cut & our plans work to a charm but the enemy now knows our purposes & hastens above, fells trees into the narrow headstreams, cuts the side levees, disperses the waters & defeats our well conceived plans.

Who can carry on a war thus? It is terrible to contemplate: & I say that no intelligent officer in this or any American army now in the field but would prefer to have his opponent increased twenty—Yea, fifty percent—if the internal informers & spies could be excluded from our camps . . . if the people could only see as I see the baleful effects of this mischievous practice they would cry aloud in indignant tones. We may in self defense be compelled to take the law into our own hands for our safety or we may bend to the storm and seek a position where others may take the consequences of this cause. I early foresee this result & have borne the malignity of the Press—but a day will come & that not far distant when the Press must surrender some portion of its freedom to save the rest else it too will perish in the general wreck. . . .

I know I could have easily achieved popularity by yielding to . . . outside influences but I could not do what I see other popular officers do: furnish transportation at government expense to newspaper agents & supply them with public horses . . . [and] give access to official papers which I am commanded to withhold to the world till my Employer has benefit of them. I could not do these things & feel that I was an honest man & faithful servant of the Government, for my memory still runs back to the time when . . . an officer would not take a government nail out of a keg on which to hang his coat or feed his horse out of the public crib without charging its cost against his pay. . . .

Again the habit of indiscriminate praise & flattery has done us harm. Let a stranger read our official reports & he would blush at the praise bespattered over Regiments, Divisions, and Corps for skirmishes & actions where the dead & wounded mark no serious conflict. . . .

I have departed from my theme. My argument is that newspaper correspondents and camp followers, writing with a purpose & with no data, communicate facts useful to the enemy and useless to our cause & calculated to impair the discipline of the army & that the practice must cease. We cannot appeal to Patriotism because news is a salable commodity & the more valuable as it is, the more pithy and damaging to our cause. . . . The law gives me the means to stop it & as an army we fail in our duty to the Government, to our cause, & to ourselves when we do not use them.

The newspapers had upbraided Sherman not only for incompetence and insanity but also for what they considered a disregard for his men and a willingness to sacrifice them heartlessly. Nothing incensed Sherman more than this. "Among all the infamous charges," he wrote to friends in St. Louis, "none has given me more pain than the assertion that my troops were disaffected, mutinous, and personally opposed to me. This is false, false as hell. My own division will follow me anywhere. . . ." As indeed Sherman's troops were to prove to the nation time and again. To Senator Ewing, in his long letter of 17 February, Sherman wrote:

Every soldier of my command comes into my presence as easy as the highest officer. Their beds & rations are as good as mine & certainly no General Officer moves about with as little pomp as I. They see me daily, nightly, hourly along the picket line afoot, alone, or with a single orderly or officer, whilst others have their mighty escorts and retinue. Indeed I am usually laughed at for my simplicity in this respect. . . . Many a solitary picket has seen me creeping at night examining ground before I ordered . . . [the men] to cross it & yet other lazy rascals ignorant of the truth would hang behind, sleep, or crouch around the distant campfire till danger was passed, and then write how Sherman with insane rashness had pushed his brave soldiers into the jaws of death. . . . When I praise I mean it & when troops fall into disorder I must notice it, but you may read my reports in vain for an instance when troops have kept their ranks and done even moderately well but I have encouraged them to a better future. . . . I know that in trouble, in danger, in emergencies the men know I have patience, a keen appreciation of the truth of facts & ground equaled by few, and one day they will tell the truth. . . .

Throughout the war Sherman, like all in high command, was besieged by petitioners appealing for all manner of benefits. He disappointed many, cutting them short, which probably prompted the Cincinnati *Commercial* to judge him proud and haughty. From this charge, too, Sherman defended himself to his foster father:

Abrupt I am, & all military men are. The mind jumps to its conclusions & is emphatic, & I can usually divine the motive of the insidious cotton speculator, camp follower, & hypercritical humanity seeker before he discloses his plans & designs. An officer who must attend to the thousand & one wants of thirty thousand men besides the importunities of thousands of mischievous camp followers must need be abrupt unless the day can be made more than twenty-four hours long. A citizen cannot understand that an officer who has to see to the wants and necessities of an army has no time to listen to the usual long perorations & I must confess I have little patience with this class of men. . . .

Two days after delivering his deposition against the press, Sherman learned that a military court had found Thomas Knox not guilty of the charge of giving intelligence to the enemy, or of being a spy. The court did find him guilty of willfully disobeying Sherman's order by accompanying the army down the Mississippi (although it "attaches no criminality thereto") and of causing his dispatch to be printed in the *New York Herald* without the sanction of the general in command (as required by War Department General Order No. 67, 26 August 1861). Accordingly Knox was sentenced "to be sent without the lines of the army, and not to return under penalty of imprisonment."

The *New York Herald* was among the strongest supporters of Lincoln's Administration, and the paper appealed at once to the President, who countermanded the sentence on the condition that Grant, Sherman's superior, agreed. Grant would not. He told Knox that only if Sherman himself gave his consent would Knox be allowed to remain. Knox therefore was forced to appeal directly to the man he had defamed. He was proud and formal: "I should be pleased to receive your assent in the present subject matter," adding an expression of his "regret at the want of harmony between portions of the Army and the Press. . . ."

Sherman must have taken some pleasure in writing his answer. "Come with a sword or musket in your hand, prepared to share with us our fate . . . and I will welcome you as a brother and associate; but come as you now do, expecting me to ally the reputation and honor of my country and my fellow-soldiers with you as the representative of the Press which you yourself say makes so slight a difference between truth and falsehood and my answer is Never!"

Sherman thanked Grant for handling Knox's request as he had. The court's decision had been less than a clear-cut victory in Sherman's eyes, but he satisfied himself with the realization that the trial and then banishment of Knox had a sobering effect on other correspondents, some of whom voluntarily abandoned the Vicksburg area. Sherman went on to play a prominent role in the campaign, his 15th Corps carrying out prodigious forced marches. In the final push against Vicksburg, Sherman's corps occupied the right flank of the encircling Federal army. The indiscretion of the press would cause Sherman no serious harm again until the campaign in North Carolina. . . .

On actually commencing his famous march from Atlanta to the sea [in November 1864], Sherman severed his contacts with the North, breaking all railroad and telegraph communications with the rear. . . .

There still were months of fighting ahead for Sherman, and once he was in communication again with the North, he again had to deal with the indiscretion of the press. He had written to Phil Ewing from Pocotaligo: "I still threaten the newspaper men with instant death as spies and they give me a wide berth. They manage to go along, but not in that dictatorial way they used to. They are meek and humble enough. . . ."

But soon thereafter the *New York Tribune* provided significant and timely intelligence to the Confederate general W. J. Hardee when the paper announced to its readers that Sherman next would be heard from about Goldsboro, North Carolina, because his supply vessels from Savannah were known to be rendezvousing at Morehead City, North Carolina. Because of this, Sherman was forced to fight a battle at Goldsboro he had hoped to avoid. It was said that he later refused an introduction to Horace Greeley, publisher of the *Tribune*, reminding him that his paper was responsible for the Union casualties suffered at Goldsboro.

An exhaustive study in the *American Historical Review* many years after the Civil War confirmed what the generals knew all along—that "copy for the papers underwent no sifting to eliminate contraband news, for we find casualty lists with full data as to the location of military units, statements of expected reinforcements, revelations of the amount of force commanded by various generals, speculations as to plans, reports of the location and strength of batteries. . . ."

Henry Villard, the Civil War correspondent who gained a respected reputation in his long career as a journalist and publisher, has left us a surprising assessment of Sherman's wartime stand against the press. In his memoirs, published almost 40 years after the war, Villard wrote: "I did not, of course, agree with him at the time as to my own calling, but candor constrains me to say that I had to admit in the end that he was entirely right. For what I observed . . . must lead any unprejudiced mind to the conclusion that the harm certain to be done by war correspondents far outweighs any good they can possibly do. If I were a commanding general I would not tolerate any of the tribe within my army lines."

The Civil War had already been over for ten years when D. Appleton & Co. brought out in two volumes *Memoirs of General William T. Sherman by Himself.* It became a best-seller. In all this voluminous work Sherman devoted a scant 15 lines to the press; they revealed no significant change in the opinions he held during the war. Writing of the harm done by newspapermen, he concluded: "Yet so greedy are the people at large for war news, that it is doubtful whether any army commander can exclude all reporters, without bringing down on himself a clamor that may imperil his own safety. Time and moderation must bring a just solution to this modern difficulty."

Notes

1. Portions of this and all the following letters that Sherman wrote in the field—some with many abbreviations and repetitions—were edited by Mr. Ewing for the sake of clarity.

This article, here abridged to focus on General Sherman's attitude to and relations with the press, appeared in its original form in the July/August 1987 issue of *American Heritage*, pages 24–41. It is reprinted here with the kind permission of *American Heritage*.

.... 3

El Salvador and the Press: A Personal Account ....

By John D. Waghelstein

Some years ago, so the story goes, an Army officer was ruminating with a newspaperman about the press and the biased reporting emanating from Vietnam. The correspondent, an old hand, acknowledged the occasional lapses in objectivity and admitted that the press too "had their Calleys and their My Lai's."

During my 25 years of military service, I've met a number of journalists, most of whom have served their profession well. They were not hopeless romantics enamored of guerrilla chic, nor did they see themselves cast in an adversarial role à la Watergate. The vast majority sought to "get it right" as opposed to getting something on somebody.

My experience in El Salvador, however, provided some examples of bad journalism, as opposed to bad press. The latter was something we lived with because of the nature of the insurgency in El Salvador and our flawed allies, but inaccurate or one-sided stories and bad reporting did add to our problems.

In El Salvador, the war is being fought by the government to retain popular support and is supported by the United States through economic and military aid. U.S. public opinion and congressional support have therefore become key pressure points and targets for the insurgents' propaganda efforts.

31

This situation has given the press a good deal of leverage in influencing that support. At the time of my assignment to El Salvador in 1982 as Chief of the U.S. Military Group, there was an obvious lack of balance in the press coverage. Many of the stories were written from within guerrilla-controlled areas, and some of the eyewitness accounts had a pro-guerrilla bias. There was little coverage of El Salvadoran army operations and virtually no interviews with the U.S. military trainers. The problem was exacerbated by a lack of cooperation by the El Salvadoran armed forces, which viewed the press as the enemy, and by the U.S. Military Group's penchant for avoiding the press like the plague. With the exception of the Ambassador, no one was talking to the press on background, for nonattribution, or for the record.

Steps needed to be taken to improve the sorry state of press relations, both with the Military Group and with the Salvadoran forces, as well as to achieve more balanced coverage of the war. Toward those ends, the Embassy Public Affairs Officer asked me to conduct a series of one-on-one backgrounders with a few of the more respected journalists. These meetings grew in number, and it soon became obvious that some other method had to be found to give the press corps what it wanted. An informal weekly press session evolved. My rules for working with the press were simple: always tell the truth and if a question was too sensitive, say so. These weekly sessions, usually an hour to an hour and a half in duration, were attended by 10 to 15 correspondents from both the print and the electronic media. Through these sessions, good Salvadoran commanders were spotlighted, problems were discussed candidly, tactics and strategy were examined, and the goals of military assistance in general were outlined. Press coverage soon began to differentiate between various Salvadoran military leaders, and members of the press became more conversant with guerrilla warfare and counterinsurgency techniques.

The El Salvadoran military's suspicion of the press took a little longer to overcome. An incident involving an NBC camera crew demonstrates the problem. I had attempted to get the crew into an operational area to talk to a departmental commander and film the Salvadoran forces in action. Several phone calls and a safe-conduct letter signed by the Salvadoran Chief of Staff seemed to have prepared the way for the trip. However, the commander kept the crew waiting for several hours, and finally, in frustration, the crew returned to San Salvador. Again telephone calls were made and again the crew headed north. This time it was permitted into the area, but its members were subjected to a long session of verbal abuse and accused of being "all a bunch of communists." The commander refused to cooperate, and the NBC crew left without filming the story, returning to the city in an understandably uncharitable mood. The commander was eventually transferred, and press relations with the Salvadoran military eventually improved, but the incident points out the problems faced by officers of El Salvador's high command who have come to understand the importance of better press relations but are dealing with officers who haven't seen the light.

It took months of work with the Salvadoran forces to begin to turn this attitude around. We tried another tack. By exposing the U.S. trainers and the U.S. training effort to the press, we were finally able to demonstrate to the Salvadorans the value in telling the real story. NBC specials aired in August 1982, April 1983, and August 1983; a *Life* magazine story in March 1983; several ABC and CNN reports; and a number of accurately written newspaper accounts of the war helped to alleviate Salvadoran suspicions. Additionally, changes in the Salvadoran Public Affairs Office helped considerably.

An example of the improved situation occurred in April 1983 when an NBC correspondent and a camera crew were permitted to enter the artillery brigade base at San Juan Opico to film the U.S. Mobile Training Team at work. After some initial reluctance, the commander permitted the crew to film the training, as well as his own unit's activities in medical civic action including a maternity ward, outpatient clinic, and other activities in his small but well-run hospital. When NBC aired a balanced account as a result, it did much to assuage Salvadoran military fears regarding the press. This positive first step did not immediately undo the damage done by other, less-objective journalists. The list of real professionals is too long for inclusion here, but both the print and electronic media were well served by many correspondents who demonstrated a high degree of professionalism and objectivity, as well as healthy skepticism. They brought honor to their calling.

On the other hand, a few correspondents were slipshod in their reporting, were advocates for a point of view, or became dupes of a very sophisticated enemy. For example, on 11 January 1982, just prior to my arrival, *The New York Times* published an "exposé" of alleged U.S. Army Special Forces' involvement in the torture of guerrilla prisoners by the Salvadoran military. The story was based on a single source who claimed to be an eyewitness to the torture. The story was categorically denied by the Embassy, but the image of U.S. military involvement in torture continued to haunt us. European left-wing newspapers and FMLN press releases continued to repeat the account; even as late as mid-1983 we were still seeing *The Times* quoted as a source for the charge. From everything we could determine, the story was just not true. The U.S. Military Group commander during the alleged incident has repeatedly stated that no member of the Military Group or the Mobile Training Teams ever participated in any such activity or taught the Salvadoran military any interrogation techniques that involved torture.

The same reporter later parroted the charge that the March 1982 elections were a fraud. The charges were originally made by a Loyola University philosophy professor in a letter carried by *The New York Times* on 3 June, which cited a study that had been conducted by the Jesuit-administered Central American University. Despite testimony from OAS Election Observers, the Freedom House Delegation, the German Christian Democratic Union, the European Popular Party, the Argentine Christian Democratic Party, and scores of other groups, *The Times* and its reporter perpetuated the election fraud charges in three subsequent articles.

Another example of the same reporter's work was his "exposé" of a U.S.

trainer who was allegedly leading combat patrols in violation of the Embassy's restrictions regarding the carrying of weapons. He also charged that this NCO had fired a mortar against guerrilla base camps. The story was carried in the 24 June 1982 issue of *The New York Times*. The NCO in the story was part of a two-man Strategic Site Survey Team. The team's responsibility was to visit each bridge, dam, refinery, and airfield; to make recommendations regarding the defense of each site; and to train the defenders in the use of the various weapons at the sites. One of the sites that the NCO had been charged with upgrading was the Rio Lempa railroad bridge. This bridge had become critical since a nearby bridge had been destroyed. The NCO's efforts to harden the site involved setting up mortars at the bridge so illumination and defensive fires could be employed should the bridge come under attack. He also, with the Salvadoran commander, walked the perimeter wire of the defensive position. This was the "combat operation" *The Times* reported. Papers throughout the United States carried the story on 24 and 25 June 1982. Regarding the allegation about carrying weapons, the Terms of Reference permitted U.S. military personnel to carry M-16 rifles in vehicles and aircraft but not on ground operations (one officer had been sent home in February 1982 for violating this restriction). We investigated this charge and found no grounds to support the allegation.

This was not the only time that an eager journalist believed he had caught U.S. military personnel in violation of the Terms of Reference. On another occasion, an Associated Press correspondent had requested an opportunity to accompany the Strategic Site Survey team. A reporter for UPI previously had been given the opportunity and had filed three stories on the U.S. military's role in training the Salvadorans; all werre noncontroversial and, incidentally, all were "spiked" by UPI editors. After an entire day with the team, however, the AP reporter returned and filed a story alleging that the same NCO cited in *The Times* was in violation of the Terms of Reference by carrying a bag containing an Uzi submachine gun.

The networks, too, had good and bad reporting. NBC specials on El Salvador were invariably well balanced and, if not always favorable, at least always objective, but NBC also had its problems. The West Coast Director of NBC's network news was responsible for a film story on 25 April 1982 in which a Salvadoran air force helicopter passed over an NBC press truck and fired on the camera crew standing nearby. Earlier that day in San Salvador the NBC crew had requested an opportunity to show "once and for all the kind of people we were advising." The Defense Attaché and I saw the film in the Embassy PAO's office. The tape began with the camera crew standing around a recently destroyed bridge. Some small-arms fire was heard in the background as the camera focused on the helicopter. The "Huey" made a sharp turn and circled back toward the camera crew and the bridge. As it passed overhead, the door gunner opened up with his M-60 machine gun and fired 60 to 80 rounds at the crew, who fortunately sought and found cover. The helicopter continued on, and as the members of the camera crew got back to their feet, one of them nervously asked, "Was that the helicopter or the *muchachos*?" (*Muchachos* is the local slang for the guerrillas.) There the tape ended. We were in complete agreement that the helicopter indeed had fired upon the crew, despite the presence of the clearly marked press van parked nearby. But the NBC crew also was told not to be in too big a hurry in branding the pilot as a war criminal. The crew had happened to be at a bridge destroyed by the guerrillas while the Salvadoran army was conducting a major operation in the area. Also, the small-arms fire heard in the beginning of the tape was probably coming from guerrillas firing at the helicopter. Most important, it was obvious from the crew's own comments that they at least suspected guerrillas might have been nearby. Adding all this up, it was easier to understand the pilot's reactions. These mitigating circumstances were pointed out to the NBC crew, and it left the Embassy without the denunciation of the Salvadoran military it had been seeking.

What makes this incident so unsavory is that U.S. viewers saw and heard only the helicopter firing at the camera crew, and their diving for cover. The facts of NBC's presence in a hostile area, the outgoing small-arms fire, the chopper banking in response, and, most damaging, the news team's questions as to who fired at them were omitted. Adding insult to injury, the NBC West Coast Director wrote an outraged letter to the *Los Angeles Times* about the incident, again omitting these facts.

This was but one of many instances in which crucial parts of a story were edited out. Perhaps the worst case of network editors deciding what is news occurred not in El Salvador, but in Nicaragua. The night before the Pope was to hold Mass, the Sandinista police broke up a peaceful march by the faithful in Managua. This event was covered by an ABC camera crew and correspondent. The American public never saw the story, nor did they know that the crew was manhandled, the correspondent beaten up, and the film confiscated. The whole story of what happened was never mentioned on ABC or any other network. It apparently wasn't considered newsworthy. It's difficult not to ask whether ABC would have considered the incident unimportant if it had been the Salvadoran government's troops instead of the Sandinistas who had committed the outrage.

One final vignette concerns my confrontation with a *Washington Post* reporter, an event covered by the *Columbia Journalism Review* (September–October 1982) and cited as an example of the Embassy's general hostility to the press. In one of the weekly press sessions, questions regarding the 55-man personnel limit arose. I discussed the restriction, citing *on background*, not for attribution, all the problems inherent in limiting the number of trainers, the genesis of how we had got ourselves in that predicament, and the U.S. public's preoccupation with another Vietnam. The correspondents were then asked to understand that this was a touchy area involving U.S. policy and that the Ambassador would be particularly upset if any refernece was made to the 55-man limit which cited anyone in the Embassy as a source. Only one reporter did not honor this request. Predictably, when his story broke in *The Post,* the Embassy Public Affairs Officer and I were summoned to the Ambassador's office for a "counseling session." After the PAO, Don Hamilton, explained the situation, the Ambassador was somewhat mollified and the matter was dropped. An opportunity to confront the *Post* reporter occurred at a Fourth of July reception at which I was probably less than friendly. My pique was not with the reporter's point of view, but with the lack of professionalism he had displayed in not honoring a source. The *Columbia Journalism Review* in its account lamented the status of Embassy-press relations; but the problem, in my view, was a particular reporter, not the press generally. Most of the correspondents were professional, open-minded, and honest.

In my opinion, the basic problem was the absence of balance by some reporters. In addition to a lack of understanding of guerrilla warfare, some reporters exhibited a lack of criticism of the guerrillas and a lack of skepticism regarding the guerrillas' prime source, "Radio Venceremos," which, along with the guerrillas' military leaders, has never been subjected to the kind of cross-examination U.S. and Salvadoran officers have encountered. As Don Hamilton has pointed out, aggressive journalists have yet to ask the following questions of the political frontmen in the FDR (Revolutionary Democratic Front):

- What authority do you have over the FMLN?
- How do you explain the murder of legislative deputies elected by their fellow citizens?
- How do you justify the death of passengers on civilian planes?
- What is the nature of your relationship with the PLO?
- Are any or all of the FMLN leaders communists? Which ones? When can I meet any one of them?
- How do you explain the FMLN's killing of 23-year-old Linda Cancel as she and her family traveled through your territory in a converted school bus?
- How would the government you want be different from that of Nicaragua or Cuba?
- Do you agree with the strategy of destroying El Salvador's economic infrastructure? How will you replace what you have destroyed?

The U.S. press has come a long way toward more objective reporting in El Salvador, but still has a long way to go. The problem of bias may lie in the political tinge of some editors who accentuate the bias of a few reporters and negate the balance of the majority. It may be a result of the adversarial role in which some journalists see themselves cast, or it may simply fall to what one journalist told a group of observers during the March 1982 elections, "Good news isn't news." Perhaps another contributor is the cultural contempt, tinged sometimes by racism, so often unconsciously expressed by North Americans. The cartoons in the U.S. press certainly are ethnocentric. In an article in the *Atlantic* entitled "Latin America—A Media Stereotype" (February 1984), Mario

Vargas Llosa, a respected Peruvian writer, criticized intellectuals and journalists for advocating political options for Latin American countries that they would never countenance in their own societies. By doing so, they betray their doubts about the ability of Latin Americans to achieve liberty, democracy, and respect for human rights.

De Tocqueville said of the press, "I love it more from considering the evils it prevents than on account of the good it does." If the press can help prevent human rights abuses, it will have performed a noble service. Whatever balanced reporting can do to deromanticize the guerrillas, it will help to prevent an even greater evil. In addition to a need for the press to be critical of all the players, there is a need to apply some self-criticism to their own "Calleys." The U.S. Army went through the process of a board of inquiry regarding Calley. A little of the same is in order for the Fourth Estate.

The people of El Salvador deserve better than what they've had for government, and they deserve better than what the insurgents have planned for them. Our press is a watchdog, and as a citizen I applaud that role. A free press is also one of the primary differences between a totalitarian state and a free society. Our press has a duty to perform, and by and large it is performing that duty well. Our press can also continue to contribute, through solid, unbiased, professional journalism, to giving democracy a chance to work in El Salvador.

This article appeared originally in the Autumn 1985 issue of *Parameters*.

4

Soldiers and Scribblers: A Common Mission . . . .

By Richard Halloran

Ever since the invasion of Grenada in October 1983, military officers and members of the press have debated the role of the press in covering military affairs, including combat operations. At the war colleges in Washington, Carlisle Barracks, Newport, and Montgomery, as well as in other forums, that debate has roamed over the place of the press and television in American life, the pros and cons of military coverage, and how soldiers and scribblers should treat with one another. The objective has been to defuse the bitterness, rooted in Vietnam and manifest in the absence of first-hand coverage of Grenada, that has so divided two vital institutions.

Sad to report, there's not much evidence of progress. In session after session, the same questions and allegations come up from military officers and many of the same answers are given by journalists. Granted, the audiences change from year to year, but few explanations from journalists seem to be getting through. Nor is there much evidence that military concerns are getting through to editors who make day-to-day decisions.

After having taken part in about two dozen such sessions, I have come to at least one conclusion: Military people really don't know much about the press and television. Random samples in seminars of 15 people and audiences of 300 officers, mostly field grade, show that only about half have ever talked seriously with a journalist, and less than a third more than once. Few military officers have done the factual research needed to determine whether their scant experience with the press is typical or atypical; few have done the content analyses to see whether their impressions can withstand scrutiny; few have examined the First Amendment, the development of the press and television, or the roles that gatherers of news have played in the military history of the United States.

Lieutenant Colonel Gerald W. Sharpe, a student at the Army War College in 1985–86, put together a useful—and revealing—study of the experience of his classmates with the press and their consequent attitudes. Colonel Sharpe reported that "more than half the respondents (53.5 percent) had never spent more than one day with the media." He found that 69 percent had spent no time with the media during their last assignments. In addition, he wrote, "More than one half of the officers indicated that they had less than one day of training in their careers about the media and more than 71 percent had three days or less."

Thus, he concluded: "Many senior officers have had very little personal experience in a direct working relationship with the media and have had even less formal training about how the media works or its roles and missions in American society. In spite of this, they hold very strong negative views about the media."

In short, it would seem that the vast majority of military officers have vague impressions, emotional reactions, and gut feelings about the press and television but are, in fact, operating in ignorance. That is a harsh word, admittedly, but the facts would appear to justify it.

The reasons for the ignorance, which were beyond the scope of Colonel Sharpe's research, would seem to be three. First, American high schools and universities do little to teach young citizens about the function of the press and television. The schools teach political science, economics, and sociology but not much about the grease of communications that makes national institutions work. Second, the military educational system does little to teach officers about the various media. A "media day" at a war college and a half day in "charm school" for freshly minted generals and admirals are not enough.

And third, we in the press do a miserable job of explaining ourselves. As large segments of American society—military officers are far from alone in this—have recently questioned the ethics, motives, accuracy, fairness, and responsibility of the press and television, editors and reporters belatedly have come to realize that their institutions are in deep trouble. Even so, we have been slow to respond and are still, in this correspondent's view, well behind the curve.

Here, then, is one reporter's summary of the questions asked, complaints made, and allegations charged by military officers since Grenada. These are my own replies based on three years of meetings with military people, seven years of covering the armed forces, and thirty years of experience in journalism. Let it be underscored that what follows represents the views of no one else even though it takes into account what other journalists have written or said. In addition, let it be understood that the battles of the press and the armed forces over Vietnam itself will not be fought again here. With the passage of time, that conflict between officers and journalists has become less germane to the issues of the day and is being shifted, rightly, to the province of historians.

• **The Media.** Military officers and civilians alike talk about "the media" as if it were a single, monolithic, structured institution.

The institution is, in fact, quite the opposite. There is no such thing as "the media," no lockstep, all-encompassing institution, any more than there is "the military" or "the military mind." For one thing, "media" is plural, not singular. The media include an almost breathtaking diversity of channels of information. Among them are news agencies or wire services, radio, television, newspapers, weekly magazines, monthly magazines, quarterlies, books, and, in some definitions, motion pictures.

Within the realm of newspapers, there are major metropolitan papers like *The New York Times* and the *Los Angeles Times,* regional papers like the *Boston Globe* and the *Chicago Tribune,* a host of local dailies and weeklies, and not a few scandal sheets. Within newspapers are the news columns, features, analytical articles, editorials, and columnists. Radio and television include national networks and the local stations. National Public Radio and cable television add to the diversity. What is known as the trade press adds still another dimension. In the military field are, to mention but a few, *Defense Daily,* a newsletter; *Defense Week* and *Aviation Week; Armed Forces Journal International* and similar monthlies; plus quarterlies like *Parameters,* the *Airpower Journal,* and the *Naval Submarine Review.*

In sum, "the media" is a myth.

• **The Power of the Press.** Many Americans have asserted that the press and television have become too powerful. Perhaps the case most often cited is the resignation of President Nixon under pressure.

Like "the media," the power of the press is a myth. The press has *influence,* not power, and the distinction is important. Military officers have power in that they have the legal and, if necessary, the physical force to have orders obeyed. The press has neither, and cannot enforce anything.

On the other hand, the press and television exert enormous influence on the public agenda by what they select to publish or broadcast and what they choose to ignore. In some cases, a newspaper can set the public agenda for many months, as *The New York Times* did with the Pentagon Papers. Conversely, newspapers are often criticized by vested special interests for ignoring their particular causes, both right and left.

The determining factor in what is published and what is withheld is that elusive thing called news judgment. It is perhaps the most difficult element to define in all journalism. News judgment is a combination of deciding what the public needs to know, wants to know, and has a right to know. News judgment derives from an editor's or reporter's sense of history, experience, point of view, taste, and that intangible called instinct. It is, and journalists should acknowledge this freely, a subjective judgment on which two journalists will often disagree. Differing news judgments are the cause of differing front pages or differing ways in which an article is written. The saving grace is that, over time, extreme news judgments do not survive because competition provides a check and balance.

Regarding the press and President Nixon, history shows that the press, notably *The Washington Post,* influenced the public agenda by bringing the Watergate caper to public attention and by continuing to dig into the story. But there came a time in that episode when the press ran out of steam because it lacked the authority to issue subpoenas or to force testimony. The issue then passed to the Congress and the courts, following constitutional procedures, and it was those institutions, not the press, that forced Mr. Nixon to resign.

▪ **Right to Know.** Many military officers hold that the concept of "the people's right to know" is not in the Constitution and has been made up for the convenience of the press.

Most journalists would argue that the people's right to know is implicit in the First Amendment and was among the basic reasons the Founding Fathers adopted the amendment. Just where the explicit phrase originated is not clear, but among the earliest references to it is one from an Army officer, Brevet Major General Emory Upton, who wrote a book after the Civil War titled *The Military Policy of the United States.* In that work, General Upton sought to explain the lessons of the war and to seek improvement in the nation's military posture. In the introduction, he made a signal contribution to the understanding of the First Amendment:

> The people who, under the war powers of the Constitution, surrender their liberties and give up their lives and property have a right to know why our wars are unnecessarily prolonged. They have a right to know whether disasters have been brought about through the neglect and ignorance of Congress, which is intrusted with the power to raise and support armies, or through military incompetency. Leaving their representatives free to pay their own salaries, the people have a right to know whether they have devoted their time to studying the art of government.

▪ **Motives.** In Colonel Sharpe's research, he found that "written comments on the chief causes of the conflict between the Army and the media reveal a basic distrust of the media's motives and objectives." In discussions, many officers have asserted, "You do it for the money." Or, in a more general allegation, "Everything you do is just to sell newspapers."

The first charge, to be candid, is laughable and on a par with saying that an officer joined the Army to get rich. A few television personalities, to be sure, drive to the bank each week in armored cars. Generally, salaries on major publications are behind those in the military service, given equivalent education, age, and time on the job. On smaller publications, salaries are far behind.

Young men and women become journalists for many reasons. Among them are a curiosity about the world, the chance to travel and to meet all sorts of people, and the opportunity for personal recognition. The newspaper byline is like the insignia of rank worn on an officer's shoulders. The unpredictable excitement and the driving pace appeal to many journalists, and the competition turns most on. For some, reporting and writing are ways of helping to set a national or state or local agenda and thus to influence the life of the republic, which is a form of public service.

On the second point, most publications exist on what is known as the three-legged stool of news, circulation, and advertising, a concept that appears little understood outside of journalism. The critical leg is content. To be successful, a publication must provide something people want to read or believe they need to read. Because different people want or must read different things, different publications cater to different audiences. Conversely, if a publication does not provide what people want or need, it will fail. The journalistic graveyard is full of monuments to publishers and editors who did not understand that point.

The provision of good or necessary or useful reading material is what builds a subscription list or newsstand sales, which add up to circulation. Because advertisers want to reach those same readers, they buy advertising space. In another little-understood point, it is the sale of advertising space, not the sale of newspapers, that provides far and away the largest part of a publication's income. That income, in turn, pays for salaries, travel, newsprint, and the other costs of publishing a paper.

The same cycle is true of television—content, viewers, advertising time— and of magazines. Only the wire services, which carry no advertising, earn their income from the sale of their product.

A legitimate question is whether a publication can be controlled by advertisers. In large publications, with many diverse advertisers, the answer is no. Local newspapers are more susceptible to pressure from a few dominant advertisers. But if the content of the paper is so good the community will not do without it, even smaller papers can withstand pressure from advertisers.

Critics assert that the press and television are merely commercial enterprises, implying that they should not have the place given them under the First Amendment. But that argument overlooks the reality that a news enterprise in America's capitalistic society must earn money to do its job. The alternative is government ownership. Down that road, as history has shown amply, lies the sort of totalitarian regime found in the Soviet Union.

- **Ethics.** At the Air War College, an officer rose in the auditorium to ask, "What a lot of us have on our minds is: Do you guys have any ethics?"

The answer is yes.

Reflecting the independence of the press invested by the First Amendment, there is no sweeping code of ethics imposed on the press from the outside. Each publication or network fashions its own, some of which is written, other of which is understood. Professional groups, such as Sigma Delta Chi, have canons that have been published as voluntary guidelines.

At *The New York Times,* for instance, there is a thick file of policies, like case law, that has accumulated over the years. For example, top management recently circulated a memo updating the policy on conflicts of interest. No reporter may write about a company in which he or she has invested, or cover an institution with which he may be remotely connected. Business reporters may not trade or play the stock market. An education reporter may not run for the school board nor a political reporter for the city council. A sportswriter may not accept free tickets. Military correspondents should not own stock in a defense industry. No one may accept a gift or take a junket.

Beyond that are individual ethics learned from parents, teachers, churches, and role models. Like motives, they vary by person, with some journalists working with unquestioned integrity and others, unhappily for the craft, skating on thin ethical ice.

• **Professionalism.** The allegation holds that journalists, unlike doctors, lawyers, and military officers, are not professionals.

In a narrow sense, that is true. In keeping with the First Amendment, journalists are not licensed by government in the manner of the traditional professions. The practice of journalism, moreover, is a highly skilled craft, perhaps even more art than science.

In the best journalists, professionalism is an attitude, a cast of mind, an instinct, and a demonstration of skill at reporting, writing, and explaining with integrity, accuracy, and fairness. The finest compliment one journalist can bestow on another is to say that he or she is a "pro." Conversely, to be labeled an amateur is to be scorned; unfortunately, journalism today has its share of amateurs.

• **Accountability.** A corollary to the questions of ethics and professionalism is the allegation that unlike military officers, the press is not accountable. Some assert that the press is irresponsible.

While members of the press and television are not accountable in the formal manner of military officers, they are definitely held accountable through a network of public opinion, constitutional and legal restraints, competitive pressures, and company policy. In many ways, the press is held as accountable as any institution in America, and perhaps more so, given its visibility. The people to whom a newspaper is most accountable are its readers. If they don't like what the paper reports, they stop reading it. If they don't like a TV news anchor, they switch him off. The comment is often made that nobody elected the press, which is true. But the press is voted on more than any other institution in America, and journalists more than any elected official. A daily newspaper or television network faces the voters every day, and is given a thumbs up or thumbs down. If the thumbs continue to turn down, the journalist can be out of a job or the newspaper out of existence.

Second, the First Amendment, while broadly written, is not absolute and has been refined by the Supreme Court. Justice Oliver Wendell Holmes, an eloquent defender of the First Amendment, wrote perhaps the most famous and most useful test of freedom of speech and the press in the case entitled *Schenck* v. *the United States*. He said:

> The character of every act depends upon the circumstances in which it is done. . . . [T]he most stringent protection of free speech would not protect a man in falsely shouting fire in a theatre and causing a panic. . . . [T]he question in every case is whether the words used are in such circumstances and of such a nature as to create a clear and present danger.

Libel laws, especially under recent court rulings, impose marked restraints on the press, particularly with regard to accuracy. Other checks come from competitors. A newspaper making a mistake can be almost certain that it will be corrected the next day in the opposing paper. Head-to-head newspaper competition, unfortunately, has declined in recent years because papers have failed or been merged with more successful publications. Even so, the various media compete with one another; *The New York Times* considers ABC News and *Time* magazine to be as much the competition as *The Washington Post* or *Newsday*.

Lastly, individual reporters are held accountable by their employers. Minor mistakes, if they are few, are tolerated in an imperfect world, but glaring or frequent mistakes are not. Janet Cooke, who wrote a fictitious story for *The Washington Post*, and Foster Winans, who fed inside information from the *Wall Street Journal* to a stock broker, no longer work in journalism.

▪ **Inaccuracy.** The allegation is that the press all too often just doesn't get things right.

This is probably the single most legitimate complaint among all of those heard. The press and television are rampant with errors of fact, many of them minor, such as getting an officer's rank wrong, or misquoting him slightly but enough to change the meaning of what he said, or leaving out an important qualifier that would have put the event or speech into perspective.

It is the accumulation of small errors, moreover, that has so eroded the credibility of the press today. Worse, many editors and reporters are cavalier about it, passing off errors as inevitable given the amount of information that is gathered, collated, and printed against daily deadlines.

Mistakes are made for a multitude of reasons. Reporters may hear things wrong, or fail to check or follow up. An inexperienced reporter, like a second lieutenant or ensign, may not have understood the nuances of what he has heard or seen. Editors, whose view of the world often differs from that of their reporters, may insist that a story be written to conform with their views. Copy editors may make careless changes, cuts, or insertions that change facts and meaning, or allow the error of a reporter to slip by.

The culprits are mostly time and competition. There is a daily rush to judgment in which facts are assembled and decisions are made by reporters and editors with one eye on the clock. It is common for a reporter to learn something at 4:00 P.M., to have one hour to check it out and gather more facts, to begin writing at 5:00 P.M., and to finish a 1000-word article at 6:00 P.M.

After that, a senior editor may have 15 minutes to scrutinize the story for general content and a copy editor 30 minutes to get it ready for the printer. That is not much time.

Interestingly, and perhaps paradoxically, the public seems to forgive big errors more readily than small ones. The episodes involving Janet Cooke and Foster Winans are seen as aberrations; Cooke and Winans are seen as dishonest journalists who deliberately did something wrong but who do not represent the vast majority of journalists.

But readers and viewers, rightly, do not forgive mistakes of omission or commission, especially when the report is about something on which they are informed. Do we hear about it? You bet. There is always a reader out there who scrutinizes the paper with a dictionary in one hand and a microscope in the other, who takes considerable pleasure in catching the newspaper in the wrong and calls to say so. But, if truth be told, their admonitions are all too often received politely and then brushed aside with little lasting effect.

• **Slanted News.** Many military officers charge that much in the press is not objective and thus is unfair.

What is said to be slanted news, however, often depends far more on the reader than the writer. It is a question, in the worn analogy, of seeing the bottle half empty or half full. Perhaps the objective way would be to describe the 16-ounce bottle as holding eight ounces of liquid and letting the reader decide for himself.

That is inadequate, however, when the writer seeks to explain what is going on. Increasingly, the role of journalism in America is not merely to describe what's in the bottle but to explain why and how it got that way and what it means to the community or the republic. What was once called "interpretive journalism" has gotten a bad name because of abuses. Today, many journalists seek to practice what might be called "explanatory journalism," which means assembling facts in a way that makes sense to a reader and then explaining them. Enter the element of judgment, which immediately puts the reporter on a slippery slope, with few ever being surefooted enough to traverse it all of the time without taking a fall.

That reporters are not objective is partly true because no human being is fully objective. Each has a point of view that derives from his upbringing, education, and experience. That becomes a set of values that a journalist applies to his work. Some journalists covering military affairs, for instance, believe that military power is needed to protect the United States in a rough-and-tumble world. Others believe that military power is evil and if the world were rid of it, prospects for the survival of the human race would be more promising. The point of view that a journalist brings to his or her work thus does much to determine what he or she chooses to cover and how. The journalist who thinks that military power is necessary will focus on one set of facts, while the journalist who dislikes military power will assemble a different set of facts. It should be said here that the "journalism of advocacy" found primarily in the "alternative press" is anathema to professional reporters.

Stripping a reporter of his point of view would be impossible, but good reporters acknowledge, to themselves and in the copy, that there are other points of view. It is there that balance, perspective, and fairness come into the writing. Achieving that balance may be the hardest thing in journalism, and the journalist only deceives himself and his reader if he thinks he does a good job of it every day.

- **Bad News.** A common cry: "You never print anything but bad news."

That is only partly true. Like slanted news, whether news is good or bad is determined far more by the reader or viewer than by the reporter. A headline reading "Nixon Resigns" may be bad news if the reader is a conservative Republican but good news if he is a liberal Democrat. Conversely, the headline "Reagan Wins Reelection by Landslide" is considered good by Republicans, not so good by Democrats.

Moreover, few people remember the good news. A suggestion for a war college research paper: Establish criteria as to whether news is good, neutral, or bad. Take the main news section of any newspaper for a month and divide the articles into those categories. The majority will most likely be neutral. Then sample other officers to see which articles they remember.

The allegation is right, however, to the extent that things going wrong are newsworthy. Americans expect things to go right, and that is not necessarily news, because news is what makes today different from yesterday. Americans expect military officers to be competent, tanks to be bought at the lowest possible cost, and airplanes to fly right-side-up. Soldiers and sailors are the sons and daughters of the readers; they expect officers to care for the troops, and when that doesn't happen they want to know about it. When tanks cost too much or planes don't fly right, the readers want to know why the government has not spent their money well.

- **Invasion of Privacy.** Many Americans believe that journalists too often invade the privacy of prominent and private citizens alike.

There is some truth to this allegation, but less than meets the eye. Newspaper reporters and, more often perhaps, television cameramen set up what are known as "stakeouts" near the home of a person under investigation, or barge into living rooms at times of distress, or pursue people who wish not to be interviewed. Occasionally a reporter does not identify himself when asking questions, which is particularly reprehensible when talking with people inexperienced in dealing with the press.

On the other hand, by far the majority of people who appear on camera or who are interviewed by a reporter do so willingly. No law forces people to talk when they don't want to, save under subpoena. Curiously, for some people who have just suffered a loss, such as the death of a member of the family at the hands of a terrorist, talking through the press to neighbors and compatriots has a cathartic effect. It helps people to get their grief out where it can be handled. It may also be a trait particular to Americans that we are ready to try to comfort neighbors, though they be strangers, in an hour of need, and we want to know who is hurting. Witness the outpouring of sympathy to the families of the Marines killed in Beirut, or the hay sent by farmers in the Middle West to farmers in the South during the drought.

In addition, readers and viewers never know about the times a reporter asks to interview a person who has suffered a loss but backs off when that person says no. It happens, and often, but the only thing the reader may see is a line saying Mrs. Jones was not available.

- **Hidden Sources.** The complaint is worded something like this: "When we read you in the paper, we don't know where you got your information or whom you've been talking to."

It's a fair comment and a valid criticism. Far too much in the press and on television today is hidden in what journalists call "blind sourcing." That's especially true in reports from Washington that cite "Administration officials," "a policymaking official," "military officers," "congressional staff aides," and "defense industry executives." For all the reader knows, those sources could have been office boys answering the telephones.

While the press is primarily to blame for blind sourcing, Administration officials, military officers, and congressional staff aides who decline to speak for the record must assume some of the responsibility. More often than not, the reason for not going on the record has nothing to do with national security or government policy but has everything to do with protocol. The colonel doesn't want his name in the paper for fear the general will be upset; the general doesn't want to be quoted because the assistant secretary will be miffed; the assistant secretary thinks the secretary or even the White House should be the source.

Reporters, confronted with that, agree all too readily to take the information on "background," which isn't background at all but not for attribution for reasons of protocol or politics. A careful reader will notice that the vast majority of non-attributed stories come from within the government, and mostly from within the Administration. The press thus permits itself to be used by the Administration to float trial balloons, to advocate or oppose policies without being held responsible for the comments, and to play all manner of diplomatic, political, and bureaucratic games.

Periodically, journalists in Washington try to tighten up the use of blind sourcing, but those efforts have failed so far because everyone fears losing a competitive advantage. One newspaper might say it will no longer accept blind sourcing; that will last until its competitor comes out with a hot story citing "Administration sources."

- **Arrogance.** Often the charge of arrogance seems to mean bad manners on the part of reporters, and particularly reporters on television who are more visible than those in print. But print reporters are also held culpable by officers who see them in action at press conferences, whether in Washington or elsewhere.

This, too, appears to be a legitimate complaint. Reporters have been caught up in, and probably have contributed to, the general decline of civility in American life. Many reporters, especially young reporters, seem to think that acting like tough guys out of the movie *Front Page* is necessary to do their jobs. In their defense, and it is admittedly a lame defense, reporters are no more rude than many lawyers, government officials, policemen, bicycle riders, secretaries, business executives, and diplomats.

Even so, the reporter who often asks the best and toughest questions in a Pentagon news conference, Charles Corddry of the *Baltimore Sun*, is a gentleman who rarely raises his voice and is consistently courteous. In his time, Mr. Corddry has skewered the most evasive senior political and military officials with penetrating questions that have left them mumbling like schoolboys. But it has been done in a civil manner.

- **Liberals.** The allegation is that the media are controlled by liberals.

That must come as a shock to the *Wall Street Journal*, the *Los Angeles Times*, the *Chicago Tribune*, the *Washington Times*, the *Manchester Union Leader*, the *San Diego Union*, and several hundred other papers, not to say *U.S. News and World Report* and the *National Review*. Columnists such as William Safire of *The New York Times*, James J. Kilpatrick and George Will, whose work appears in *The Washington Post*, and William Buckley, whose views appear not only in *National Review* but in other outlets, must be amused.

There are several problems with the allegation that liberalism runs rampant in the press. First, few people agree on what a liberal is; definitions run from 19th-century liberalism to 20th-century socialism. Second, even a 1981 study by two academicians, Robert Lichter and Stanley Rothman, didn't make the case that what they called the "media elite" was heavily liberal. They found that barely half of the reporters considered themselves liberal, that the vast majority took conservative economic positions such as favoring private enterprise, and that many reporters were liberal primarily on social issues such as civil rights. A 1985 survey by William Schneider and I. A. Lewis in *Public Opinion*, published by the conservative American Enterprise Institute, addressed a more important question: "Do readers detect any bias when they read their daily newspapers?" The authors concluded: "Not really. . . . There is no evidence that people perceive the newspapers they read as strongly biased to the left." In a similar study in *Public Opinion*, Barbara G. Farah and Elda Vale asserted: "The professional standards of journalism dictate that no one gets a break. Ask George McGovern, Edward M. Kennedy, or Geraldine Ferraro whether liberals are treated with special solicitude by the press."

Put another way, if the press is so pervasively liberal, how come Ronald Reagan won 49 of 50 states in the 1984 election?

- **Operational Security.** Many officers assert that the presence of the press during a military operation jeopardizes security.

That is an allegation without basis in historical fact. An examination of the record in World Wars I and II, where there was censorship, and in Korea and Vietnam, where there were guidelines but no censorship, shows that rarely did the press endanger operational security. In Vietnam, Barry Zorthian, long the government's chief spokesman, has said he knows of only a half-dozen instances in which a correspondent broke the guidelines; three of those were inadvertent.

The record is not perfect. A wire service report once disclosed a Marine fire direction team's position in the mountains behind Beirut during the conflict in Lebanon. That did jeopardize the operation and perhaps the lives of those Marines, and it should not have been printed. The dispatch could have been written in a way such that the facts were made known without giving information useful to an adversary.

Over the long run, however, the record shows that with a modicum of common sense, consultation, and planning, military forces can preserve operational security while correspondents go about their jobs. At the end of a long discussion of this issue at the Naval War College, a retired admiral asserted: "Operational security is not the issue. The issue is that when you write about us, you make us look bad."

The admiral had it exactly right—operational security is not the issue.

- **Classified Information.** Perhaps no single question is raised more, and with more heat, than the allegation: "You print classified information."

Right. The press has published classified information in the past and will in the future. For one thing, the classification system is almost a farce, is abused for political and bureaucratic reasons that have nothing to do with national security, and thus breeds contempt. For another, there are laws and court decisions that govern what may and may not be printed and the press is obliged to operate within those constraints, but they do not cover most classified information. Third, responsible publications are keenly aware that the release of sensitive information—which is not the same as classified information—could jeopardize lives, operations, intelligence sources, or technical capabilities.

Legally, it is important to understand that there is no law authorizing the classification of information, or forbidding the publication of classified information. The classification system is based in executive orders, the latest being Executive Order 12356, signed by President Reagan in April 1982. By definition, executive orders apply to members of the executive branch, and to no one outside it. A journalist or any other citizen, therefore, breaks no law by disclosing classified information.

Several narrowly written laws apply to journalists as well as to other citizens. One is found in sections 793 through 798 of Title 18 of the *U.S. Code*, forbidding the disclosure of intelligence gained by communications intercepts. Another is the law that forbids the public identification of intelligence agents. A third is in certain sections of the Atomic Energy Act pertaining to nuclear weapons.

What about the espionage laws? The Association of the Bar of the City of New York recently did a study of that statute, which forbids the unauthorized disclosure of information to a foreign nation with the intent to do harm to the United States. In its report, the association said: "We conclude that prosecution under the espionage laws is appropriate only in cases of transmission of properly classified information to a foreign power with the intent to injure the United States or to aid a foreign power."

Note several phrases: The association said "properly classified information," not just any classified information; "to a foreign power," not to American citizens, voters, and taxpayers; "with the intent to injure the United States," not to foster the public debate on serious issues confronting a democratic republic.

The association went on to say: "Other uses of the statutes, such as prosecution of the media or those providing information for the sake of public debate, are inappropriate."

What about moral obligations? The journalist, indeed, must deal with serious moral obligations when he gains access to sensitive information that, if disclosed, would cause jeopardy to life, the security of troops, a piece of military technology, or a valuable intelligence source. The crux comes when the disclosure would cause direct, immediate, and irreparable damage. It would not make any difference whether the information was classified, but whether the disclosure would do genuine harm.

This view is rooted in the doctrine of "clear and present danger" enunciated by Justice Holmes and reinforced by other court rulings. In *Near* v. *Minnesota*, Justice Charles Evans Hughes said that in time of declared war, "no one would question but that a government might prevent . . . the publication of sailing dates of transports or the number and location of troops." In the case of the Pentagon Papers, one justice wrote that publication of national security information could be prohibited if the government could show that it would "inevitably, directly and immediately cause the occurrence of an event kindred to imperiling the safety of a transport at sea." Two other justices, in a concurring opinion, said the government must present proof that disclosure "will result in direct, immediate, and irreparable damage to our nation or its people."

There have been instances, not generally known because of their sensitive nature, in which journalists have withheld information that, if published, would have caused a clear and present danger. Several reporters in Washington, for instance, knew that American hostages had taken refuge in the Canadian Embassy in Teheran in 1979. To have printed that would surely have put those Americans in danger. *The New York Times* and other publications made a deliberate effort to determine which passengers aboard the hijacked TWA airliner in Beirut were military personnel so that their identity could be kept *out* of the paper. In another case, newspapers and networks for many months withheld information about the Central Intelligence Agency's attempt to raise a Russian submarine with the ship *Glomar Explorer*. Some of those decisions not to publish were made by editors who applied common sense and the standard of clear and present danger, while others were made after consulting with government authorities.

Editors have not always made the right decisions, but over the years many publications have been far more careful than anyone in the government has been willing to concede. Conversely, the government has failed to level with the press or has cried wolf so often that it has lost credibility. Both political parties have been guilty; it is not a partisan matter.

On classification itself, many journalists have little regard for the system because it is mindless. According to the 1985 report to the President from the Information Security Oversight Office, the latest report available, the Department of Defense alone made 22,322,895 original and derivative classification decisions that year. Of those, 446,458 were to classify something top secret.

Such numbers, on the face of it, are absurd. There are not nearly half a million things so secret that the disclosure of them would constitute a clear and present danger to the United States, nor would disclosure cause grievous damage to the national security. Justice Potter Stewart once wrote: "For when everything is classified, nothing is classified, and the system becomes one to be disregarded by the cynical or the careless, and to be manipulated by those intent on self-protection or self-promotion."

As an example of mindless classification, the following paragraph was taken from a Navy budget document classified secret; the paragraph itself was also classified secret. It said, in full:

> The Navy must continue to attract and retain sufficient numbers of high-quality, skilled and motivated people. Compensation and quality of life improvements must be competitive in the job market. Ways must be found to reduce requirements for administrative functions, reduce personnel turbulence and permanent change of stations moves.

Had this paragraph been printed on every recruiting poster in the nation, it would not have harmed the national security.

Note, too, that complaints from government about classified information in the press usually describe the leak as "an unauthorized disclosure." In the eyes of many government officials and military officers, "authorized disclosure" is permissible if it serves their purposes. But that poses two different sets of ground rules, one for government, the other for journalists. Few journalists are willing to play in that rigged game; when the government cleans up the system and plays by the same rules it wishes to impose on journalists, then perhaps the system can be made to work.

- **Leaks.** An Air Force lieutenant colonel suggested that military people were baffled by leaks. "Just how does a leak work?" he asked.

The popular notion of a leak is a "Deep Throat" who signals a reporter with a flowerpot and then meets him draped in a black cloak in an alley in the dark of night.

Not so. Most leaks occur in the light of day in the office of a senior political official or military officer, or someone on their staffs. The cliché holds that the ship of state is the only vessel that leaks from the top. It is a cliché, but it is also true. Relatively few leaks come from dissidents outside the government. Or, as a British official put it: "Briefing is what I do, and leaking is what you do."

A professor at Harvard, Martin Linsky, recently did a survey of nearly 1000 senior officials who held office from the Johnson through the Reagan Administrations, and interviewed 38 officials and journalists. From that, he concluded that 42 percent of the officials had at one time or another leaked information to a journalist. Professor Linsky also thought the percentage was really higher, saying: "Some who did would presumably not admit it and others would define their leaks narrowly enough so as to exclude their own practices."

The officials gave a variety of reasons for leaking: to counter a false report, to gain attention for a policy, to develop a good relationship with a reporter, to send a message to another branch of government, to undermine another official's position, to inform other officials and the public of a policy decision, to divert attention from another issue.

Stephen Hess, of the Brookings Institution, who has studied the operations and foibles of the press in Washington, identified six kinds of leaks in his book, *The Government/Press Connection:* the policy leak or pitch to gain or to erode support; the trial balloon, which discloses a proposal under consideration to see who supports and who opposes; the ego leak, in which the leaker shows off how important he is and how much he knows; the goodwill leak, in which the leaker hopes to accumulate credit with a reporter for use later; the animus or grudge leak that seeks to damage the reputation or programs of an opponent; and the whistle-blower leak, usually the last resort of a person who has been frustrated in getting changes inside the government.

One more should be added, the inadvertent leak, sometimes called a tip. It happens when a source drops a hint that flags a reporter that something newsworthy is going on. The reporter then uses that to lever out more information elsewhere. This happens more often than is realized, and the original leaker may never suspect whence the tip came.

Lastly, rarely do leaks appear in the paper as the leaker intended. Most good reporters, knowing that leaks are self-serving, seek more information from other sources before going into print. Moreover, reputable newspapers do not print pejoratives from an anonymous source. Either the source puts his name on it or it's not fit to print.

- **Reporters Lacking Military Experience.** Many officers complain that reporters, mostly young people, have not served in the armed forces and therefore are not competent to cover them.

The criticism does not hold. Capable reporters learn to cover politics without running for office, or business without having been entrepreneurs, or education without having taught school. Similarly, lawyers defend clients without having themselves stood trial and doctors treat patients for diseases they themselves have not suffered.

However, a military reporter who has served in the armed forces can have an advantage over a competitor who has not. The reporter who has served may have a grasp of military culture and lingo that escapes his colleague and may have the credentials to establish rapport with military sources more easily. Remembering which end of the rifle the bullet comes out has rarely hurt a military correspondent.

On the other hand, the ranks of journalism today are full of reporters, editors, and producers who have been in military service—and hated every minute of it. They would not necessarily make better military correspondents than the reporter who has not served, and would not be welcomed by military sources.

• **Taking Up Time.** An Army major in a military-media seminar leaned back from the table and said: "You're a pain in the ass. A media visit is more trouble than an inspection by a three-star general."

Maybe so. But that is a self-inflicted wound, as many reporters require only a few hours of time with informed officers and some time in the field with the troops. Television may need more, as producers can be demanding when it comes to pictures.

Comments like the major's, moreover, reflect a defensive attitude and a failure to understand that military officers are accountable to the voters and taxpayers through a variety of channels. The press is one of them—only one, to be sure, but still one of them.

Further, such comments indicate a failure to understand a principle of military life, especially in a democratic nation: The armed forces of the United States cannot long sustain a military operation without the consent and, indeed, the vigorous approval of the American people. Of all the lessons Americans should have learned from Vietnam, surely that must be high on the list.

It would be far better, for the nation and the armed forces, if officers looked more positively on the rare occasions they are called upon to deal with the press and saw them as opportunities to build support in the public. It should also be seen as a chance to show off the troops, who almost always like the attention they get.

In sum, talking with many journalists *is* worth an officer's time. It is also among his duties, and will become more so as he rises in rank.

• **The Press in World War II.** The allegation is that the press today is different from what it was in 1945.

Right. So are Army officers, Navy pilots, lawyers, doctors, and Indian chiefs, butchers, bakers, and candlestick makers. The whole world is different today, making the comparison rather silly. Just as every other institution in America has changed, so have the media. Television, the speed of communications, the education of reporters, and the demands of readers are but a few of the differences.

Former Secretary of Defense James R. Schlesinger likes to assert that "the age of Ernie Pyle is dead." But that is another myth, for there never was an age of Ernie Pyle, the legendary correspondent of World War II who carved out a unique place covering the grunts. Ernie Pyle, who was killed in the Pacific just before the war ended, had the luxury of writing about the grunt's-eye view of the war because hundreds of other reporters covered the daily news of the war.

Moreover, Ernie Pyle rarely covered what he called "the big picture" and thus was not confronted with the issues that military correspondents today must handle. He made his name writing about the relatively simple, focused existence of men in combat, not about the complexities of the military budget, or quality controls in defense plants, or whether women should be permitted in combat, or the mysteries of nuclear warfighting.

Reed Irvine, a critic of the press who runs an operation called Accuracy in Media, regularly lambastes journalists for not going to the field with the troops. The charge does not hold up—witness the number of reporters who were with troops in Vietnam, with about 60 getting killed and several winning combat decorations. Beyond that, Mr. Irvine and others who applauded the exclusion of reporters from Grenada can't have it both ways. Journalists can't be faulted for not being with the troops if the high command blocks them out.

  • **Lack of Patriotism.** Occasionally an officer or a civilian has charged that members of the press are unpatriotic because they uncover incompetence, fraud, lies, or other wrongdoing in government. Secretary of Defense Caspar W. Weinberger has come close to charging the press with treason and with giving aid and comfort to the enemy. Patrick Buchanan, the director of communications for President Reagan, questioned the loyalty of the press to the nation when details of the Iran-Contra affair were exposed.

Such accustions bear a tone of self-righteousness, as if to say that only the speaker is loyal to America and anyone who disagrees with him is unpatriotic. That attitude might be better suited to a Tory who believed in the divine right of kings than to an American with moral and intellectual roots in the Revolution's struggle for freedom from an oppressive government.

Accusing the press of disloyalty also betrays a lack of faith in the robust democracy that is America, the last best hope for human freedom on the face of the earth. Ours is an open society dedicated to the proposition that honest debate and dissent and a healthy distrust of the power of government are the order of the day. As an Irishman, John Curran, said in 1790, "The condition upon which God hath given liberty to man is eternal vigilance."

In a sense, soldiers and scribblers share a common mission. Under the Constitution, soldiers are charged with maintaining a vigil against external threats; journalists are charged with vigilance against internal enemies who would corrupt and destroy our way of life.

Contrast, for instance, the American handling of Watergate and the Soviet Union's handling of Chernobyl. It is a point overlooked that Watergate proved, perhaps more than anything else in the 20th century, the strength of the American political system. America was able to withstand the shock and to have a peaceful transition of power that few other nations would have experienced. The Soviet Union, where the press is an arm of government, dealt with the accident at the nuclear power plant by trying to hide it from the Russian people and the world. In those cases, it would seem undeniable that the American press served American citizens far better than TASS, *Pravda,* and *Isvestia* served the Russians.

To close on a personal note, I do not question the patriotism of other Americans—and I do not permit anyone to question mine. If we cannot have that as a basis for treating with one another, then we as a nation will have lost something that makes America what it is.

∎ ∎ ∎ ∎ ∎ ∎

Correspondence

To the Editor:

Richard Halloran, a highly respected and knowledgeable newsman, is off the mark in his article "Soldiers and Scribblers: A Common Mission." Recognizing that there is bitterness between the military and the press, rooted in Vietnam and perpetuated by Grenada, Halloran writes that the fundamental problem is that military people don't know much about the press. (The word "media" will not be used here, since Halloran tells us "the media is a myth.") His discussion excuses the excesses of the press, ranging from its power and influence to its lack of accountability, inaccuracies, arrogance, printing of classified information, lack of ethics, slanted news, etc. His theme is that military officers are simply ignorant about the way the press works and why it works that way. As a result, military officers don't trust the press. Implicitly, he assumes that if we understood the press and television, we would trust them.

The problem is not ignorance. Halloran suggests that since most military officers have never talked to a journalist, they have no basis in fact to complain. He misses the point. Military officers are trained to focus on results. Their judgments have been made based upon reading newspapers. Most readers make judgments about the press on the same basis, and consequently have given the press relatively low ratings in recent polls. Like most Americans, the military officer reads newspapers every day and turns to radio and television as sources for news. For the most part, he is not satisfied with the quality of such news, especially regarding matters about which he is knowledgeable and which are of importance to the military. Halloran is probably right when he observes that this current bias goes back at least to Vietnam, when those war college officers who gave the press bad marks in the survey he cites were lieutenants and captains. Back then these officers were doing exactly what they were supposed to do, and doing it well, while newspapers and television programs throughout the country said they weren't. There is little doubt that a legacy of mistrust of news people exists within the military and is being passed on. There is also ample evidence that a similar legacy of mistrust of the military is being passed on among news people. Moreover, there is little that the press seems to be doing to change that. In fact, the press hasn't changed, fundamentally, for many years.

The situation Halloran describes in 1987 could easily have applied to the 1968 Tet Offensive: "the press and television are rampant with errors of fact ... many editors and reporters are cavalier about it ... an inexperienced reporter may not have understood ... editors insist that stories be written to conform to their views . . . there is a daily rush . . . copy editors make careless errors or changes or insertions that change facts and meanings," etc. All too often the results are, sadly, distortion and more distortion over time. Journalists use their news outlets' inaccurate files for background on current events—events being inaccurately reported; often as not, journalists are not reporting about events, but about what other journalists have reported; and over time, a file of inaccurate stories becomes another inaccurate record of events.

The nostalgia about the good relationship between the press and the military in World War II exists because the press didn't foul up military operations—and they didn't try to. The press seemed to take the attitude in those days that they might be helpful in achieving the objectives set by the nation. One of Halloran's most indefensible paragraphs deals with the leg-endary Ernie Pyle. Halloran notes that Pyle "had the luxury of writing about the grunts'-eye view of the war because hundreds of other reporters covered the daily news of the war." Halloran is correct in that hundreds of others were covering the news of the most devastating war in history. But they also did it in a way that did not undermine winning the war.

Halloran writes that Pyle "was not confronted with the issues that military correspondents today must handle. He made his name writing about the relatively simple, focused existence of men in combat, not about complexities of the military budget, or quality controls in defense plants, or whether women should be permitted in combat, or the mysteries of nuclear warfighting." To counter James R. Schlesinger's lament that "the age of Ernie Pyle is dead," Halloran replies that "there never was an age of Ernie Pyle."

Does Halloran seriously believe that Ernie Pyle, who lived with and wrote about the U.S. military in the Pacific until he was killed in 1945, had an easier job than the journalist of today who writes about whether women should be permitted in combat? If so, the rift between the military and the press may be much deeper than any of us ever imagined.

Halloran writes that "journalists are charged with vigilance against internal enemies who would corrupt and destroy our way of life." Is he serious? On the day that I write this, in *The New York Times* the President of the United States took more heat than any internal enemy. In fact, not a single story could be found with a lead assailing an "internal enemy who would corrupt and destroy our way of life." There were few stories, for that matter, that had much to do with *external* enemies who would corrupt and destroy our way of life. The combined leadership of the Warsaw Pact got less ink over the past six weeks than Liberace got in one day.

Who are these internal enemies who would corrupt and destroy our way of life? Are they the senior officials in the Administration who objected to taking into their confidence 600 or so reporters—to include representatives of Larry Flynt publications, *Rolling Stone* magazine, and over 130 foreign outlets—based on the concern that some of those reporters would give advance notice of a surprise raid in Grenada or muck up initial operations in a developing tactical situation? Are they the soldiers in Vietnam who, in spite of reading daily demoralizing press reports, still did what American soldiers in every American war have done—served their country?

As is often and perhaps appropriately asked, Who elected these people who are charged with such vigilance—and how do we get rid of them? Obviously, it has never entered Halloran's mind that the nation's "internal enemies" might occasionally include the Fourth Estate—those worthies who buy ink by the barrel and paper by the ton.

There is nothing improper, immoral, or unusual going on when military officers don't like the press. There is no reason why they should, and there is no reliable evidence that they ever really did. It is written in our culture and history for the government, and by extension the military, to have an adversarial relationship with the press. That was established in the Colonies as early as 1734 when the printer John Peter Zenger was acquitted on charges of libel, the court ruling essentially that a newspaper may print what is factual although it may be ruinous to an individual, in that case to the "Captain General and Govenour in Chief" of New York. Yet there are good reasons why military officers must respect the press and deal with it, albeit in an adversarial—not hostile—relationship. There is no question that the military is accountable to the taxpayer for the way it uses, or misuses, sons and daughters as well as dollars. Halloran makes a point of this and military officers accept it.

Ironically, most news about the military is "good news." Hundreds of column inches of hometown news stories on men and women in the service appear daily in newspapers across the country. There are always feature stories about the military and military people in newspapers and magazines nationwide as well.

Most of the obvious friction between the press and the military seems to arise when the press is after a "bad news" story. All too often military officers fail to heed the words of the late General Creighton Abrams, who as Chief of Staff of the Army once admonished his staff: "Bad news is not like fine wine—it does not improve with age." Nearly all the "bad news" stories that involve military officers do not deal with criminal wrongdoing or serious breaches of public trust, but rather with bureaucratic glitches and simple mistakes. In those cases, common sense dictates telling the whole story, telling it completely, accurately, and immediately. By doing so, chances for a "one-day" story are increased.

Dealing with the press is almost always a gamble because, as Halloran mentions, what is ultimately printed, regardless of information provided, is a function of the reporter, his editor, the copy editor, how much space is allotted, competing stories, and even the fog of the newsroom. Any of these factors can, and frequently do, screw up any well-presented set of facts.

The frustration of military men is highest when working with what Halloran calls "amateur" craftsmen in the field of journalism. By his own account, there are far too many in his business. Both Vietnam and Grenada were overrun with them. Nearly every local newspaper has them. Amateurs can't, or won't, get their facts straight.

Unfortunately, there seems to be little that schools of journalism and the American Society of Newspaper Editors want to do about it, even if they could. The Accuracy in Media group is making an attempt, but the circulation and influence of their newsletter is relatively small, so newspapers and television don't take it seriously. Halloran himself is derisive in his brief mention of this organization. There is, of course, no one person or organization in charge of the hundreds of American news outlets who can impose change upon them. Individual editors tend to stand behind their employees in the face of an outsider's criticism; further, they don't have the time or the inclination to worry about the kind of errors that Halloran says are "inevitable given the amount of information that is . . . printed against daily deadlines."

While identifying ignorance on the part of military people as the main source of the problem, Halloran seems confident that the inaccuracy, rudeness, arrogance, slanted news, and other "inadvertent" transgressions of the press will be corrected over time by the readership. In mitigation, he points out proudly that the American press serves the American people better than TASS, *Pravda*, and *Isvestia* serve the Soviet people. One certainly hopes so.

While vigilance in exposing internal enemies is grand, more vigilance in getting facts straight in balanced news stories, particularly those about the military, would be much more appreciated. That doesn't seem too much to ask.

Colonel John P. Yeagley, USA

The Author Replies:

Colonel Yeagley twice asks whether I am serious. The answer both times is yes. The colonel also questions the patriotism of reporters when he suggests that we might be among the nation's "internal enemies." I reject that accusation out of hand. To make more pointed what I said in "Soldiers and Scribblers," I do not question Colonel Yeagley's patriotism—and I do not permit him to question mine. Beyond that, I think I'll stand on what I wrote.

Richard Halloran

Mr. Halloran's article appeared originally in the Spring 1987 issue of *Parameters*. The correspondence appeared in the Summer 1987 issue.

........5

Soldiers, Scholars, and the Media ....

By Sam C. Sarkesian

Since the Vietnam War most military professionals have held a negative view of the American media resulting, in no small way, from their perception that the conduct of the war was taken out of the hands of military professionals and placed in those of TV journalists. These attitudes have been nurtured by the perceived role of the media in reporting such disparate phenomena as terrorist incidents, the invasion of Grenada, the defense budget, and the Iran arms affair. Although some members of the media have responded to such criticism, in the main the views of the military profession have been ignored or minimized by the media on the presumption that they are an aberration and not in accord with the general views of society. Equally important, most members of the media may be convinced that the military profession has little understanding of the media and thus holds distorted and incorrect views.[1] This unfriendly, if not hostile, relationship tends to obscure the importance of more fundamental questions regarding the military profession and the role of the media in an open system. The purpose here is to examine four such questions. Is there a media elite? Is there a media monopoly? What are the characteristics and mind-sets of the media? What do the answers to these questions reflect regarding the U.S. military profession and the American media?

We now have available a number of solid published studies of the media. The weight of evidence revealed by these studies shows that there exists a media elite with a particular political and social predisposition that places it distinctly left of center on the American political spectrum. Further, the media elite enjoys a monopoly on news-gathering and reporting, channeled through a corporate structure that gives the media elite and media corporations immense power in the American political system. Although there are contrary views, they pale in comparison to the empirical and analytical bases of these conclusions. As one group of scholars observed, "There is considerable evidence from other sources to corroborate our portrait of liberal leaning journalists."[2]

It is reasonable to conclude, therefore, that the military profession holds views generally in accord with the conclusions reached by scholarly studies of the media. And, in the main, the views of the military are compatible with those of American society. This is true even though military officers may have formed their views subjectively and intuitively. In contrast, the political and social predispositions of the majority of those in the news profession and media elite put them at a considerable distance from mainstream America. What follows is a more detailed examination of the basis for these conclusions.

The Media Elite—Mind-sets and Power

Elites are normally characterized by their perceived status in society, their relative homogeneity, the power they can command, the similarity of their political-social backgrounds, and their commonality of purpose. Underpinning these considerations is the fact that an elite tends to be self-contained and self-regulating. Further, an elite is not necessarily determined by the numbers involved, but more by the amount of power exercised in the system and relative status. While there are some exceptions, those in the media who are at the highest levels of their profession and occupy important positions in reporting the news reflect all of the characteristics of an elite. Indeed, the members of the media elite generally move in the same social circles, read the same literature, and depend on similar sources for news.[3]

In one of the most authoritative studies of the media in recent times, by S. Robert Lichter, Stanley Rothman, and Linda S. Lichter, the authors conducted

> hour-long interviews with 238 journalists at America's most influential media outlets [*New York Times, Washington Post, Wall Street Journal, Time, Newsweek, U.S. News and World Report,* and the news divisions of CBS, NBC, and PBS]. The result is a systematic sample of men and women who put together the news at America's most important media outlets—the media elite. . . . The demographics are clear. The media elite are a homogenous and cosmopolitan group . . . with differentially eastern, urban, ethnic, upper-status, and secular roots.[4]

A number of political implications result from these characteristics:

> Today's leading journalists are politically liberal and alienated from traditional norms and institutions. Most place themselves to the left of center and regularly vote the Democratic ticket. . . . They would like to strip traditional powerbrokers of their influence and empower black leaders, consumer groups, intellectuals, and . . . the media.[5]

Some members of the media argue that they are apolitical. The most authoritative studies of the media, however, based on extensive survey research, indicate the opposite. That is, the great majority of those in the media elite and in the profession as a whole tend to be left of center on the political spectrum, with the media elite decidedly so.

Generally speaking, the term *mind-set* refers to the looking glass through which an individual views the world. It reflects predispositions and norms that fashion perceptions of reality.[6] In this respect, even though some members of the media may claim that the media are not a monolith, the fact is that the media elite displays a homogeneity of views and similarity of mind-sets which considerably influence the entire news profession. The media elite tends to perceive the world through its own lens, and this is reflected in news reports, editorials, and in selecting what is to be reported on the evening news. Although there may be some questions on the linkage between the views of the media elite and the way the news is reported, it seems clear that "leading journalists tend to perceive elements of social controversies in terms that correspond to their own attitudes."[7]

Journalists perceive a world that is "peopled by brutal soldiers, corrupt businessmen, and struggling underdogs."[8] While these views may be more pronounced when interpreting domestic life, more often than not the same attitudes are the basis for interpreting world events. Similarly, this leads many in the media to view the U.S. military in negative terms.

A commonality of media attitudes was also the conclusion reached in an earlier study: "Because the *New York Times*, CBS Television News, NBC Television News, the *Washington Post*, *Newsweek*, and *Time* exercise such inordinate direct and indirect influence over opinion, it is especially significant that they tend to convey the same general viewpoint."[9]

As noted earlier, the media elite mind-set and the way that elite perceives the world are sharply different from the mind-set and perceptions of the public in general. This difference is also reflected in the attitudes of many editors and reporters. For example, the results of a survey conducted by the *Los Angeles Times* are particularly revealing. The survey indicated that the views held by about 3000 newspaper reporters and editors selected randomly from about 600 newspapers around the country were at a considerable variance from the views held by a slightly larger number of adult Americans. The portrait that emerged is one of journalists who "are emphatically liberal on social issues and foreign affairs, distrustful of establishment institutions (government, business, labor), and protective of their own economic interests."[10] Interestingly enough, the survey pointed out that there was only a slight difference between the views of the newspaper staffs and those of the higher-ups responsible for setting editorial policy. One is led to conclude that many positions taken by the media throughout the United States reflect those held by the media elite.

According to some studies, the media elite is obsessed with power.[11] But the media are also ambivalent toward power. They tend to ignore their own power, even belittle it, while being zealous in their criticism of other power-holders. This self-blindness is well documented in one study and referred to frequently in others.[12] The power of the media tends to be underestimated by the media elite and overestimated by some segments of society. In any case, it seems clear that the media have a substantial role in affecting the public. As one study concluded,

> To control what people will see and hear means to control the public's view of political reality. By covering certain news events, by simply giving them space, the media signals the importance of these events to the citizenry. By not reporting other activities, the media hides portions of reality from everyone but the few people directly affected. . . . Events and problems placed on the national agenda by the media excite public interest and become objects of government action.[13]

Another study notes, "A small number of people who work for a very small number of news organizations exercise very great influence over the news of national and international affairs received by all Americans."[14]

The ability to shape the public's image of reality and to affect its attitudes is surely a fundamental component of power. This power is reinforced by the lack of consistent and effective counterbalancing forces within the media elite. Pluralism in the American political-social system is a major factor in counterbalancing forces and in checks and balances—a basic democratic characteristic. However, the media seem to be generally free from such internal forces. This concentration and centralization not only add to the media's power, but strengthen its corporate character.

This is not to suggest that there is no internal conflict in the news profession. There is a high degree of competitiveness, including commercial competition. However, it rarely becomes institutionalized to the point of threatening the power of the media elite as a corporate body. Nor does this conflict crystallize into effective counterbalancing forces within the media.

The power of the media is considerably broadened and also strengthened with the introduction of new information technology. On that score, one report concludes,

> Essentially the same people who own and manage newspapers and television now control the new technologies. They are guided by the same elite-sanctioned values, the same desire for profit. New journalistic . . . practices and effects will flourish, but technological innovations are unlikely significantly to disrupt the structure of power or undermine its legitimacy.[15]

Media power is not a new phenomenon, of course. Writing in the middle of the 19th century, de Tocqueville observed that even with some restrictions, "The power of the American press is still immense." He went on to write, "When many organs of the press do come to take the same line, their influence in the long run is almost irresistible, and public opinion, continually struck in the same spot, ends by giving way under the blows."[16] In a modern version of de Tocqueville, one scholar describes this phenomenon as "pack journalism."[17]

The Media Monopoly and Media Miscues

The obsession with power, the character of the media elite, and the commercial nature of news reporting combine to create a media monopoly. According to Ben Bagdikian, this leads to considerable harm to the concept of fair and balanced news reporting:

> The continuing violations of the ethic of independent journalism over the years has [sic] an important message for the future: The unstated rules will be respected until they represent a threat to the power of the media corporations. When the status of . . . media corporations . . . is in jeopardy, or when the corporations believe their status is in jeopardy, no conventions, no professional ethics, and no individual protests by angered journalists will prevent corporations from using their prerogatives of ownership to protect their power by altering news and other public information.[18]

Morever, regardless of the existence of these conditions and power relationships, Bagdikian states that "there persists the illusion throughout American journalism that it operates as a value-free discipline."[19]

In sum, there is overwhelming evidence that there is a media elite that has a monopoly on the media function in American society. Further, the media elite exhibits political and social predispositions clearly separating it from mainstream America. This raises a whole series of questions regarding access to information networks by political actors, groups, or individuals who are not part of the elite and who do not share the media elite's political and social predispositions. Can such political actors gain access to the vast media network? Can they expect to be treated fairly and objectively by the media elite? One is led to believe that the answers to both questions are likely to be in the negative.

The members of the media elite, as is the case with most political actors, have made serious mistakes in judgment leading to news distortions and monumental errors. Members of the news profession are human, and like all human beings they are imperfect. Errors are to be expected. The members of the media elite, however, are reluctant to admit mistakes, and are not fond of examination by outsiders. Indeed, when challenged by outside critics, the media elite displays a siege mentality. For example, in a recent book by a media professional, the author writes, "The American press has a responsibility to the public. It must help keep Americans free by telling them the truth. It cannot discharge this duty by hunkering down and waiting until its attackers go away. It is time to fight back."[20]

While a siege mentality may be a trait of other professions, it is a conspicuous characteristic of the media elite. What is disconcerting is that media errors and distortions can take on a momentum of their own and become "historical fact." A classic example is the reporting of Tet 1968 during the Vietnam War. In a comprehensive study of that event, journalist Peter Braestrup concluded,

> What began as hasty initial reporting of disaster in Vietnam became conventional wisdom when magnified in media commentary and recycled on the hustings in New Hampshire, in campus protest, and in discussions on Capitol Hill. The press "rebroadcast" it all uncritically, even enthusiastically, although many in the news media should have known better.[21]

The author concluded that "the general effect of the news media's commentary coverage of Tet in February-March 1968 was a distortion of reality—through sins of omission and commission—on a scale that helped spur major repercussions in U.S. domestic politics, if not in foreign policy."[22] For a number of military men in Vietnam during the Tet Offensive, it must have been ironical to win a military victory, have it reported by American journalists as a defeat, and have those reports accepted as fact by many Americans. Military men are likely to agree, therefore, with one observer writing in the early part of 1970:

> During the last decade the media elite has acted, at worst, as if it were waging a studied propaganda campaign against the United States in foreign affairs. At times it has acted as if it viewed itself as a neutral agent between the United States and its enemies. . . . It has largely ignored specific foreign tactics, rather apparently designed to use our own news media against us.[23]

The now famous 1984 case of General William Westmoreland and CBS is another example of media miscues. According to Don Kowet,

> The CBS documentary had charged a Westmoreland-led conspiracy. Just as the military had anticipated, although fifteen years delayed, CBS had gotten the story wrong, by relying on a paid consultant whose account of events was tailored by his own bias, by allowing a producer to avoid or discard interviews with those who might have been able to rebut the documentary's premise, and by ignoring documents in its own possession which tended to cast doubt on that thesis.[24]

Regarding the Westmoreland case, one study concludes, "It shows how a single viewpoint, that of the executive producer, can shape the facts to conform to his own version of the truth."[25]

History is replete with such examples. In the Janet Cooke affair, for example, the reporter had written a heart-wrenching story about "Jimmy," an eight-year-old drug addict living in Washington, D.C.[26] Written in 1981, the story earned a Pulitzer Prize. Subsequently, it was found that the story was a fabrication and the Pulitzer was withdrawn. *The Washington Post* had little choice but to publicly admit its error. But many were left wondering how an error of such magnitude could have occurred in a major newspaper proclaiming professional rigor and close editorial supervision. This episode was particularly disconcerting given the fact that the newspaper has significant influence in shaping public attitudes.

More disturbing is the view that "the media elite advocacy of certain viewpoints and policies produced an additional new problem. Having diagnosed complex public problems, and having taken unequivocal public positions on them, they apparently wish to demonstrate that they were right. They have substantial journalistic and moral stake in proving their own rightness."[27] Some members of the media have responded to such criticism. One type of response, based on the First Amendment, castigates media critics for their anti-constitutionality. In such instances, the defense of journalists is based primarily on the freedom of the press, interpreted broadly as "the people's right to know." True, some in the media do spotlight the profession itself and try to come to grips with internal problems. As one noted media professional, Robert MacNeil, commented,

> I think there is, frankly, scorn for fairness in some journalistic quarters. . . . There is an attitude common in the media that any good journalist can apply common sense and quickly fathom what is right and what is wrong in any complicated issue. . . . Coupled with this attitude is one in which a reporter or camera crew acts as though their presence, their action in covering a story, is more important than the event they are covering.[28]

Yet, many in the media are inclined to brush aside such criticism by simply saying, "We don't make the news, we only report it."

A broader concern among journalists, perhaps, centers on manipulation. The media have been wary of being used or manipulated by various political actors, particularly in government. The use of leaks and testing the waters by "unnamed sources" is a common technique. Various administrations have been noted for such manipulation. But there are a variety of reasons for leaks, ranging from those prompted by disgruntled bureaucrats to those from opposition members in Congress. Members of the media elite are quite conversant with these methods and many times allow themselves to be used. There is also some evidence to support the notion that members of the media themselves manipulate the news. As noted earlier, members of the media elite tend to interpret events as fashioned by their own political and social dispositions.

The role of the media during the Kennedy Administration is a case in point. According to an authoritative chronicler of the Kennedy era, John H. Davis, the media virtually idolized the Kennedy family, with distortion the result: "Kennedy's phenomenal grace and charm belied an administration whose style was hardly peace-loving. The discrepancy between image and reality was due principally to the press."[29] In the aftermath of Kennedy's assassination, the media seemed to be out of touch with reality. Davis notes, "Along with the glorification of John F. Kennedy, there went also his continued idealization and sentimentalization. If the press had gushed over John Kennedy before, it now became downright maudlin. The canonization had begun."[30]

Economist Holmes Brown makes a particularly strong case with respect to news distortion and manipulation. In the article "TV Turns Good Economic News into Bad," he concludes: "The national economy improved dramatically during 1983—but you might not have realized it if your only source of information had been the nightly news programs of the three major television networks."[31] Similar conclusions were reached in an earlier study showing how media coverage of the 1968 presidential campaign and U.S. policy toward Vietnam, among other matters, was slanted to conform to the general views of the media.[32]

The sources referred to here do not exhaust the list of available studies, nor do their interpretations and conclusions necessarily preclude others. Yet, these sources provide powerful support for the notion that the media are far from being the virtuous profession claimed by their elite spokesmen, and far from being balanced and fair in news interpretation and presentation. Though without deliberate design, the media critics tend to reinforce much of the military professional's own view.

With respect to the disapprobation of the media expressed by military officers, it may well be that it goes much deeper than the familiar concerns of suspect patriotism and irresponsibility in operational security matters. Rather, the real concerns of military officers rest on the more fundamental questions of news balance, fairness, compassion, and sincerity. Military men see these qualities missing in today's military reportage, in stark contrast to the situation prevailing during "the Ernie Pyle era" of World War II. In this deeper sense, then, their concern is not with levels of news coverage, but trustworthiness on the part of newsmen.

The question of trustworthiness was measured by a Gallup Poll taken in July 1986. The poll assessed the public's trust and confidence in ten key American institutions. The military was rated highest, with 63 percent of the respondents giving it a confidence rating of "a great deal" or "quite a lot." In sharp contrast, the American people showed much less confidence in television and newspapers, with ratings of 27 and 37 percent respectively. While such polls may change over time, the 1986 poll left no doubt about the public's confidence with respect to the military and the media. Six institutions out of ten were rated above newspapers, with television rated tenth—that is, last—in public confidence and trust.

Beyond the Surface, Beyond the Front Page

Clearly, there is more to the media and their role in American society than addressed here. Further, there is a great deal more to explore regarding the view of the military profession. One does not have to meet or know a reporter or TV journalist, however, to assess the political consequences of news reporting. Reporters and TV journalists are met every day by anyone who reads newspapers and watches the nightly TV news. Of course, any serious effort to examine the media must include a critical reading of the existing literature. Such examinations must include, for example, a study of the First Amendment and its application to the media, and the concept of "the people's right to know." The issues of U.S. national security and media responsibility also deserve detailed study.

Similarly, to understand the military, with its special responsibility, requires a serious study of the military profession. This cannot be achieved simply by serving a few years in the Army or Navy while waiting to get out. It requires critical mastery of the important literature as well as thorough and continuing practical knowledge of the national and international security arenas, the military professional, military life, and the military system. Too few of the media elite have accomplished this.

Solutions to problems arising out of the relationship between the military and the media require understanding the challenges, dilemmas, and responsibilities facing both the military and the media. Understanding may be better achieved by not expecting a "solution," since this presumes that there is a fixed answer, relevant for all times, and that there is a beginning and an end to a particular problem. The dynamics among political actors in American politics and the constantly changing political climate make the search for solutions to a "proper" media role elusive, if not misguided. The most one can expect is a dynamic relationship, with episodic attention to power relationships and demands for accuracy and balance.

In the modern era, with all its technological innovations, the media elite will surely play an even greater role in agenda-setting and in shaping public attitudes. At the same time, opportunities will increase for news distortions and political biases in selecting what to report. The media elite will be increasingly vulnerable to such conditions, and these conditions will place an increased burden on the news profession. It is a profession wrought with challenges and dilemmas, and increasing pressures for balance and fairness. It is difficult, indeed impossible, to achieve absolute objectivity, particularly when individuals are trying to gather and report news under pressures of time and events. But at the minimum, we should expect—and demand—that the members of the media elite recognize their own characteristics, predispositions, and weaknesses, the commercial imprint on news reporting, and their influence over the news profession.

In the final analysis, it is well to remember the words of de Tocqueville: "I admit that I do not feel toward freedom of the press that complete and instantaneous love which one accords to things by their nature supremely good. I love it more from considering the evils it prevents than on account of the good it does."[33]

Notes

1. See for example, Richard Halloran, "Soldiers and Scribblers: A Common Mission," *Parameters*, 17 (Spring 1987), 10–28 (reprinted in chapter 4 of this volume). See also Daniel F. Gilmore, "In the Barracks, Scorn for the News Business," *The Washington Post*, 26 August 1986, p. A15.

2. S. Robert Lichter, Stanley Rothman, and Linda S. Lichter, *The Media Elite* (Bethesda, Md.: Adler and Adler, 1986), p. 39. See also pp. 39–44; and see Dan Nimmo, *Political Communication and Public Opinion in America* (Santa Monica, Calif.: Goodyear, 1978), pp. 192–93.

3. Lichter et al., p. 299.

4. Ibid., pp. 20–21, 23, 294.

5. Ibid.

6. See, for example, Irving L. Janis, *Groupthink: Psychological Studies of Policy Decisions and Fiascoes*, 2d ed. (Boston: Houghton Mifflin, 1982), pp. 40–42.

7. Lichter et al., p. 295.

8. Ibid., p. 95.

9. Peter B. Clark, "The Opinion Machine: Intellectuals, The Mass Media and American Government," in Harry M. Clor, ed., *The Mass Media and Modern Democracy* (Chicago: Rand McNally, 1974), p. 48.

10. As quoted in Lichter et al., p. 43. See also Sam C. Sarkesian, *The New Battlefield: The United States and Unconventional Conflicts* (Westport, Conn.: Greenwood Press, 1986), pp. 264–65, 283, n. 20.

11. Lichter et al., pp. 110–14. See also Thomas E. Patterson and Robert D. McClure, *The Unseeing Eye: The Myth of Television Power in National Elections* (New York: G. P. Putnam's Sons, 1976), p. 75; and Ben H. Bagdikian, *The Media Monopoly* (Boston: Beacon Press, 1983), pp. 3–28.

12. Lichter et al., pp. 103–8, 120.

13. Patterson and McClure, p. 75.

14. Clark, p. 41.

15. David L. Paletz and Robert M. Entman, *Media Power Politics* (New York: The Free Press, 1981), pp. 253–54.

16. Alexis de Tocqueville, *Democracy in America,* ed. J. P. Mayer, trans. George Lawrence (Garden City, N.Y.: Anchor Books, 1969), p. 186.

17. Doris Graber, "Media Magic: Fashioning Characters for the 1983 Mayoral Race," in Melvin G. Holli and Paul M. Green, eds., *The Making of the Mayor, Chicago, 1983* (Grand Rapids, Mich.: William B. Eerdmans, 1984), p. 68.

18. Bagdikian, p. 224.

19. Ibid., p. 133.

20. Peter Stoler, *The War Against the Press: Politics, Pressure and Intimidation in the 80s* (New York: Dodd, Mead, 1986), pp. 207–8.

21. Peter Braestrup, *Big Story: How the American Press and Television Reported and Interpreted the Crisis of Tet 1968 in Vietnam and Washington* (Boulder, Colo.: Westview, 1977), I, xxxiii. For another journalist's view of the Vietnam War, see Michael J. Arlen, *The Living Room War* (New York: Penguin Books, 1982).

22. Braestrup, p. 184.

23. Clark, p. 76.

24. Don Kowet, *A Matter of Honor: General William C. Westmoreland versus CBS* (New York: Macmillan, 1984), p. 301. See also Renata Adler, *Reckless Disregard: Westmoreland v. CBS et al.; Sharon v. Time* (New York: Knopf, 1986).

25. Lichter et al., p. 153.

26. See Janet Cooke, "Jimmy's World," *The Washington Post*, 28 September 1981, p. A1; Editorial, "The End of the 'Jimmy' Story," *The Washington Post*, 16 April 1981, p. A18; and David A. Maraniss, "Post Reporter's Pulitzer Prize Is Withdrawn," *The Washington Post*, 16 April 1981, p. A1.

27. Clark, p. 71.

28. Robert MacNeil, "Why Do They Hate Us?" *Columbia Magazine* (June 1982), p. 17.

29. John H. Davis, *The Kennedys: Dynasty and Disaster 1848–1984* (New York: McGraw-Hill, 1984), p. 464.

30. Ibid., p. 609.

31. Holmes M. Brown, "TV Turns Good Economic News into Bad," *Chicago Sun-Times,* 11 March 1984, p. 6.

32. See, for example, Edith Efron, *The News Twisters* (New York: Manor Books, 1972).

33. De Tocqueville, p. 180.

This article appeared originally in the September 1987 issue of *Parameters*.

........6

Terrorism, the Media, and the Government......

By L. Paul Bremer III

It is 6:22 A.M. on 23 October 1983 in the parking lot of Beirut International Airport in Lebanon. A large yellow Mercedes truck with a swarthy, bearded man at the wheel is racing at high speed directly at the chain-link gate guarding the entrance to the 24th U.S. Marine Amphibious Unit's headquarters compound. Passing through the gate before the guard can fire, it plunges on, finally stopping in the open atrium lobby of the commandeered terminal building where the Marines are quartered. Six tons of high explosives in the truck detonate, vaporizing the terrorist driver, collapsing the four-story steel and concrete building in a pile of rubble, killing 241 Marines, and injuring scores more.[1]

Such terroristic acts present a direct threat to the interests of the American government and its personnel. From 1980 through 1986 the U.S. military was the target of over 250 terrorist attacks. During the same period, American diplomats and diplomatic facilities worldwide were targets in 228 attacks. Close to 5000 international terrorist attacks occurred during that seven-year period, which means that a U.S. military or diplomatic establishment was attacked about every five days and a terrorist incident occurred every 12 hours. These statistics do not include the fatal attacks in October 1987 on two U.S. Air Force

73

sergeants and one retired U.S. Air Force sergeant outside Clark Air Base in the Philippines.[2] While many of these terrorist attacks amounted to little more than harassment, some, as in the case of the Marines, caused catastrophic loss of life. These numbers make it clear just how pervasive terrorism has become.

For me terrorism has a personal side. There are memorial plaques in the State Department lobby listing the names of American diplomats who have died in the line of duty since 1776. When I joined the Foreign Service 21 years ago, there were 81 names on those plaques. All but seven of those diplomats died from earthquakes, plagues, and other nature-induced causes. But in the last 21 years, 73 additional names of Americans serving in U.S. diplomatic missions have been added, Americans who died at the hands of terrorists. In other words, for the first 190 years of our nation's existence, the Foreign Service lost a member to violent death by human agents about once every 27 years. Since I joined, we have averaged one such loss about every 90 days.

But not just diplomats and not just military and not just Americans suffer. Terrorism occurs in most parts of the world, but it is the world's democracies that suffer most. For example, in 1986, 64 percent of all international terrorist attacks were directed against only three countries—the United States, Israel, and France.

The moral values upon which democracy is based—individual rights, equality under the law, freedom of thought, freedom of religion, and freedom of the press—all stand in the way of those who seek to impose their will or their ideology by terror. The challenge to democracies is to combat terrorism while preserving these deep democratic values. A particularly sensitive issue is the relation of the media to terrorism. While virtually all players on the international stage vie for attention and public support, terrorists are unique in the way they use violence against innocents to draw attention to a cause.

Terrorism and the Media

Terrorist threats—to our people, to friendly countries, and to democracy itself—are all made more complex by the interplay among media, governments, and terrorists. The very nature of terrorism, its desire to gain the widest possible publicity for its act, makes this complexity inevitable. Terrorists have always understood that the target was not the physical victim, but the wider audience. Their goal is to terrorize citizens in an apparently random way, so that people lose confidence in their governments' policies. Nineteenth-century Russian terrorists spoke of "propaganda of the deed." Terrorists then could not imagine the power terrorist acts would have in the day of worldwide live television broadcasts.

Many of us can remember the horror of seeing the 1972 Olympic Games disintegrate into kidnapping, flames, and murder. No doubt the Black September faction of the PLO chose to attack the Israelis at the Munich Olympics precisely because it guaranteed them a worldwide audience. How many times since then have we all been riveted to our television sets to watch some new act of barbarism unfold? But we must not fall into the trap of confusing technology with people. The medium is *not* the message. The message is what reporters and editors decide should be aired or printed. What you and I see, hear, and read about terrorism in mass media is the result of multiple decisions made by cameramen, reporters, producers, copywriters, and editors throughout the news industry. When we explore the role of media in terrorism, we are in fact exploring the judgments of dozens of individuals.

The most difficult issue involved is media coverage of a terrorist incident in progress. Because news organizations, especially electronic media, can directly affect the outcome of a terrorist incident, journalists must exercise special care and judgment. Innocent lives can be lost by even the slightest miscalculation on the part of the media. That is why it is so vital for journalists to keep certain specific points in mind as they cover ongoing terrorist incidents, the most fundamental being one borrowed from the Hippocratic oath: *First, do no harm.*

We have to assume that terrorists have access to any information published or broadcast about them and the attack they are carrying out. The hand-held television is a fact of life; any airport duty-free shop has excellent, battery-powered shortwave receivers the size of a paperback book; two-way radios are cheap and readily available. It is now possible to put a cellular telephone, a two-way radio, a shortwave receiver, and a television receiver in one ordinary briefcase.

The ability of terrorists to track outside responses to their actions in real or near-real time means that journalists are not just narrating the passing scene. They are players; like it or not, they are involved. This involvement imposes special responsibilities on journalists during a terrorist incident such as an airline hijacking. Just like those of us on the task force in the State Department's Operations Center, journalists are making decisions which can mean life or death for specific, identifiable individuals.

During hijackings and other incidents of hostage-taking, terrorists have— as during the Air France hijacking to Entebbe on 27 June 1976 and the TWA 847 hijacking on 14 June 1985—segregated victims by race, religion, nationality, or occupation. Indeed, people have been murdered on the basis of these distinctions. Obviously, news reports saying things like "22 of the 72 passengers are American citizens" provide information which can be useful to terrorists and deadly for hostages. Even revealing the exact number of hostages can be valuable to terrorists. Six of the American employees of the U.S. Embassy in Teheran spent several weeks hiding with our Canadian friends. Had the terrorists realized their absence they, too, could have been seized. Several news organizations learned of this situation and—to their credit—did not report it.

A wide range of people have suggested ways in which the media might address the problems inherent in covering hijackings and other hostage situations. Some have suggested that there be no live coverage of an incident in progress. Others have proposed formal guidelines, perhaps offered by the government, perhaps voluntarily set up by news organizations, perhaps by the two working in concert.

After considerable reflection, I believe that U.S. law and custom, our country's profound commitment to freedom of the press, and the widely varying circumstances of each terrorist incident make it impractical to develop universally accepted guidelines for the media's response to terrorism. Still, given the media's involvement in terrorist incidents, it seems to me that reporters and their editors should be asking themselves some tough questions as they cover terrorist incidents. Let me suggest eight such questions:

1. Have my competitive instincts run away with me?

Journalism is a competitive business. Everyone wants to cover the story better and, where possible, sooner than the competition. Occasionally, competitive instinct has overridden common sense. One need only look at the tapes of the Damascus "press conference" with the TWA 847 hostages to see how the pressures for a better camera angle or an answer to a question turned professional journalists quite literally into a mob.

2. What is the benefit in revealing the professional and personal history of a hostage before he or she is released?

Hostages have been known to misrepresent their marital status, professional responsibilities, career histories, and other material facts in their efforts to persuade their captors not to harm them. One former hostage is certain that the lies he told his captors saved his life. It is standard American journalistic practice to report information about victims, but in many other democratic countries that is not the case. In the unique circumstances of political terrorism, facts about hostages verified by family members or coworkers and announced publicly could have deadly consequences.

3. When reporting on the statements made by hostages and victims, have I given sufficient weight to the fact that *all* such statements are made under duress? If I decide to go ahead with the report, have I given my audience sufficient warning?

We have cases where hostages appear on television tapes making admissions or other statements in the terrorists' interests—all seemingly uncoerced and unrehearsed. Only later, after the hostages' return, did we learn that the statements had been extracted by force or threat.

4. Should I use statements, tapes, and the like provided by the terrorists? How reflective of actual conditions are the materials provided by the terrorists? How much analysis should I offer? How much speculation?

Former hostage David Jacobsen recounts the beatings he received when U.S. media reported that messages made at the direction of his captors were said to contain "hidden messages."[3]

5. How often should I use live coverage? Should I put a terrorist on TV live? Should I run an unedited statement on the air or in print? To what extent will I serve the terrorists' purposes by so doing?

One of the things that distinguishes terrorism from other crimes is the use of real or threatened violence to amplify and advance a political position. Few news organizations run more than brief excerpts of statements by anyone but the President of the United States. Even then, reporting full texts of presidential remarks is limited to special occasions. Yet, ironically, when a terrorist speaks to the world, some news organizations have tended to air or print every word, every gesture, every inflection. Giving extensive coverage to terrorist statements may well encourage future acts of terrorism.

6. Am I judging sources as critically as I would at other times?

Devoting major chunks of space and time to a terrorist incident can create a situation in which it becomes difficult to generate enough solid material to "fill the hole." During terrorist incidents we have all seen reporting of what amounts to nothing more than rumor. Information based on sources responsible news organizations would not normally touch has been given broad circulation during incidents. I have seen stories which should have read something like: "According to the reports of a wire service known to be careless, a newspaper noted for its irresponsibility has reported that anonymous sources in a rumor-plagued city have said. . . ."

7. Should I even *try* to report on possible military means to rescue the hostages?

A particularly reprehensible practice by some news organizations is trying to discover and publish reports on the movements of military forces during a terrorist incident. Such reporting can only end up one of two ways: either the report is correct and the news organization runs the risk of having served as an intelligence source for the terrorists; or the report is wrong, in which case it may unduly complicate the resolution of the incident. This subject deserves special attention. Reports on military activities designed to surprise or thwart an armed foe should be just about as secret as things get.

8. What about honest consideration for the victims' families?

One former hostage recounts how his teenage son received a telephone call in the middle of the night. The journalist calling had a question: "The latest reports indicate that your father will be executed in two hours. Any response?"[4]

It is encouraging to report that responsible journalists are paying increasing attention to the effects their actions have on terrorism. I know that some major news organizations have set up specific internal guidelines for handling terrorist incidents. It was gratifying also to note that major networks declined to broadcast a videotape made last spring by one of the hostages in Lebanon. The substance of what was said was reported, but the tape itself—obviously a cynical attempt by the kidnappers to advance their demands—was not aired.

Just as we in government must defend our Constitution without abandoning our traditional values, journalists must exercise their judgment in ways that do not jeopardize their traditional role as an independent watchdog. The media needs no prompting to resist efforts at manipulation by government. One can only urge they exercise the same care at resisting manipulation by terrorists.

How then are we to thwart terrorism? What can we as citizens, as military members, as government officials do to protect ourselves from the multiple threats of terrorism?

Our Government's Strategy Against Terrorism

Our government has essentially turned to a commonsense strategy to combat terrorism. Despite some setbacks, this program is beginning to show successes. This strategy rests on three pillars:

- First is a policy of firmness toward terrorists;
- Second is pressure on terror-supporting states;
- Third is a series of practical measures designed to identify, track, apprehend, prosecute, and punish terrorists.

The first of these pillars, no concessions, is designed to avoid rewarding terrorists. Behavior rewarded is behavior repeated, as any parent can attest. This element of our policy is sometimes misstated or misunderstood. Some believe that this policy means we will not ever talk to terrorists. This is not correct. To be precise, our policy is that we will not make concessions to terrorists, nor will we negotiate with them. But we will talk to anyone, to any group, to any government about the safety and well-being of Americans held hostage.

The second pillar, maintaining pressure on terror-supporting states, is of real importance because of the special danger posed by the state-supported terrorist. Our aim is to raise the economic, diplomatic, and—if necessary—the military costs to such states to a level that they are unwilling to pay. The U.S. air strike against Libya was in part intended to raise the costs to Libya of supporting terrorism. The withdrawal of our ambassador to Syria in the aftermath of proven official Syrian complicity in the attempted bombing of an El Al 747 in London demonstrated to Syria that we would not conduct business as usual with states that use terror as a foreign-policy tool.

There has been a growing political consensus among European governments that more has to be done to show states that supporting terrorism is unacceptable to the international community. In the late spring of 1986, several European nations imposed sanctions on Libya for supporting terrorism. Then Western European governments expelled more than 100 so-called Libyan "diplomats" and businessmen. This heavy blow to Libya's terrorist infrastructure in Europe, combined with the tightened security measures at airports and elsewhere, doubtless played a role in reducing sharply Libyan-related terrorist incidents after May of 1986. In the fall of that year, the Europeans announced a series of economic, political, diplomatic, and security-related measures against Syria, in response to which that nation improved its behavior in several important ways.

We regard terrorists as criminals. They commit criminal acts. And this brings us to the third pillar of our strategy: our effort to find and implement practical measures to identify, apprehend, and punish terrorists. These measures involve improving cooperation among countries in intelligence, police, and law enforcement matters. For example, we are finding ways to improve the collection and sharing of information on terrorists' locations, movements, and affiliations. We are now working with key allies to develop agreed "lookout" lists of known or suspected terrorists. As terrorists are identified, we can begin to track them, especially as they attempt to cross international borders. Even democratic states can require detailed identification and conduct thorough searches at border points. This is a terrorist vulnerability we are trying to exploit with some success.

We have also developed an aggressive program of cooperating with our friends and allies in the apprehension, prosecution, and punishment of terrorists. Our cooperation has gotten closer, and we are seeing results. European courts have convicted and sentenced terrorists to long prison terms. Attitudes among political leaders are changing.

Finally, we have dramatically upgraded our military capability to respond directly to terrorist activities in a wide variety of international settings. The U.S. Special Operations Command, a unified command, was activated on 1 June 1987 with headquarters at MacDill Air Force Base, Florida. Designed to deal with low-intensity conflict, including terrorism, this command has components from each of the services, including the Army's 1st Special Operations Command headquartered at Ft. Bragg, North Carolina. This Army command embraces a Special Forces group, Ranger regiment, Civil Affairs battalion, Psyop group, Military Intelligence battalion, the 160th Aviation Group (the "Night Stalkers"), and the highly secret Delta Force. The 160th Aviation Group's superspecialized helicopters have already proved their mettle in the Persian Gulf in operations against the Iranians. The Army component, in combination with elements from the Navy's SEAL teams and the Air Force's 2d Air Division, constitute a formidable counterterrorist capability indeed.[5]

In my many trips to Europe, both before and after the Iran/Contra revelations, I encountered no diminution of enthusiasm for working together to counter terrorism. There is a palpable sense of dedication among the intelligence, police, airport security, customs, and immigration officials involved in fighting the terrorist threat. I believe that this growing cohesion in the world's democracies is having an effect, that we are in a position to carry out our strategy and reduce the level of terrorism around the world. No one, of course, can promise a world free of terrorism. History makes it clear that the use of violence to intimidate others is not likely to disappear. What we can confidently state, however, is that we have a concrete plan for dealing with terrorism and that we are seeing some heartening results.

Notes

1. Eric Hammel, *The Root: The Marines in Beirut August 1982–February 1984* (San Diego: Harcourt Brace Jovanovich, 1985), pp. 287–95.

2. Marc Lerner, "3 Americans murdered in Philippines," *Washington Times*, 29 October 1987, pp. A1, A12.

3. Remarks by former hostage David Jacobsen, 4 March 1987, during conference titled "The Hostages—Family, Media, and Government," at Hotel Washington, Washington, D.C.

4. Ibid.

5. Kenneth Brooten, Jr., "U.S. Special Operations Command," *Journal of Defense & Diplomacy*, 5 (No. 10, 1987), 21–23; John M. Collins, *Green Berets, SEALs, and Spetsnaz* (Washington: Pergamon-Brassey's, 1987), pp. 21–23, 32–37; Eric C. Ludvigsen, "The Army's 'Night Stalkers' in the Persian Gulf," *Army*, 37 (November 1987), 14, 16.

This article appeared originally in the March 1988 issue of *Parameters*.

........7

Military-Media
Relations Come
of Age ....

By Barry E. Willey

On 27 October 1983, two days after D-Day, the first group of journalists—a media pool to be precise—landed on the island of Grenada to cover what combat actions remained. These 15 journalists were understandably perturbed for having been excluded from the first two days of action. They were anxious to learn and report firsthand what was happening on that heretofore unremarked "isle of spice."

No plans had been made to include the media in Operation Urgent Fury. When the decision was made at the highest levels of the U.S. government to allow a pool from the nearly 400 journalists waiting on the island of Barbados to fly to Grenada, it fell to the Public Affairs Team of the 82nd Airborne Division to coordinate support for the pool and arrange for as much access as possible within operational security constraints. As more journalists arrived and the area of operations gradually opened to all media, reporting of military operations on Grenada became widespread and, for the most part, accurate. Not all the action was over when the journalists arrived. The first group witnessed portions of a major Ranger airmobile assault on the Calivigny Barracks complex, including a massive artillery preparation of the objective. Another pool on 29 October drew sniper fire during a tour of the Frequente warehouse area, where stacks of arms and ammunition were being stored.[1]

Much has happened since Operation Urgent Fury regarding media coverage of U.S. military actions, and military-media relations have improved significantly in terms of cooperation and understanding. It has taken long months of work, planning, and interaction between the media and the military to achieve such improvement. Most significant in this evolution was the formation of the Sidle Panel following Grenada to review military-media relations and determine the feasibility of institutionalizing media participation in future training and contingency deployments of U.S. forces. In response to the panel's recommendations, the military created the Department of Defense national media pool program. To date, a pool has been deployed on eight occasions to cover training deployments of U.S. forces around the country and the world, including the March 1988 "show of force" to Honduras.

In July of 1987, after the tragic Iraqi attack on the USS *Stark* in the Persian Gulf and the decision to reflag Kuwaiti tankers with the Stars and Stripes, the Department of Defense deployed the media pool to cover the use of U.S. forces, which involved the escorting of the first reflagged Kuwaiti tankers through the Strait of Hormuz, into the Persian Gulf, all the way to Kuwait. Though the passage through Hormuz and into the Gulf was relatively uneventful, the 10-member media pool and their military escorts from the Department of Defense and U.S. Central Command witnessed the ominous and widely reported mine strike near the end of the transit by the supertanker *Bridgeton* on the 24th of July.

The plan for that pool deployment, including elaborate ground rules, was established by the Pentagon and the U.S. Central Command—the unified command responsible for U.S. forces deployed in the Persian Gulf, Gulf of Oman, North Arabian Sea, and the surrounding region. The ground rules were understood and accepted by all pool members before embarking on any U.S. Navy vessel. They included the need for a security review of all pool material at the source before release of news products to any interested media. The public affairs escorts would conduct the security reviews and expedite the dispatch of pool products (audio, video, print, still photos) from the ships by all feasible means. Two print reporters in that pool—Mark Thompson, Knight-Ridder Newspapers, and Tim Ahern, Associated Press—wrote accounts of their experiences in the *Columbia Journalism Review* (November/December 1987) and the *Washington Journalism Review* (October 1987), respectively. They expressed concerns about delays in transmission of pool reports, censorship of pool products, and difficulties in getting pool products ashore in a timely manner, among others. In fact, all pool products were reviewed for security and changes were recommended, if warranted. Premature release of operational information puts U.S. lives at risk. There was concern by military escorts about the propriety of a potentially embarrassing reference within a pool print report, but it had nothing to do with security and was left in the story. Every attempt was made to get pool products ashore quickly. In one case, as AP's Ahern mentions in his article, one of the U.S. warships delayed its scheduled movement while waiting to rendezvous with a vessel sent to pick up media reportage.

The pool deployment was not devoid of problems, but despite the complaints by members of the pool and some of their editors and bureau chiefs in Washington, the pool deployment was a success. Ahern said, "As far as I'm concerned, the pool's chief test came Friday, after the *Bridgeton* hit the mine. The story I filed was the first word released at the Pentagon."[2] Knight-Ridder's Thompson commented: "First and foremost, [the pool] had been a success inasmuch as our audiences were better served for our having been there, rather than at our Washington desks, and for having covered the escort operations, albeit under unusual conditions."[3]

Because of continued interest in Gulf operations, the Pentagon and U.S. Central Command activated a DOD "regional" media pool, which rotated media representatives every three to four weeks from a base in a gulf littoral country for rapid recall and access to U.S. military operations in the region. This pool was smaller (five or six) due to the limited number and capacity of escort vessels. Primarily, it pulled correspondents from bureaus in the Gulf region. Its purpose was to continue covering transits of reflagged Kuwaiti tankers and any other significant events that might occur in the region involving U.S. forces.

But was this type of pool really feasible for the long haul and was it capable of covering hostilities, should they occur? The answer is yes. During the nine months between the first embarkation in July 1987 to the dramatic U.S. reprisals against Iranian oil platforms on 18 April 1988—47 transits and 28 media pool activations later—there was a markedly successful evolution. To better understand the media's role in the U.S.-Iranian hostilities by that date, some background leading to that event is necessary.

Early on the morning of 14 April 1988, during what was planned to be a routine embarkation of the regional media pool (consisting of AP Middle East correspondent Richard Pyle, CNN correspondent Taylor Henry, camera crew husband-wife team Steve and Anne Cocklin, and UPI photographer Tom Salyer) to cover a transit of reflagged Kuwaiti tankers, the pool boarded the USS *O'Brien* from the USS *Jack Williams*. The *O'Brien* was scheduled to escort the next northbound convoy, which would include, ironically, the supertanker *Bridgeton*.

While on the *O'Brien*, waiting to rendezvous with the Kuwaiti reflagged tankers, the pool received word by radio that the USS *Samuel B. Roberts* had struck a mine in waters of the central Persian Gulf. The pool and its escorts had visited that frigate just two weeks before, so the somber report of fires, flooding, and ten injured crewmen was hard to accept. In the short time the pool was aboard the "Sammie B.," it had become part of the ship's "family."

Based on the facts as then known, the pool's public affairs escorts drafted a statement concerning the *Samuel B. Roberts'* mine strike and provided that to the media pool. Two hours later a message arrived from the Commander, Joint

Task Force Middle East, with nearly identical information, thus validating the statement given the pool earlier. (The lesson here is that public affairs officers in the absence of official pronouncements should use available information—properly qualified!—to keep the media and the public apprised. Corrections, if indicated, can be issued later.)

The next 24-hour period was a whirlwind of logistical activity which saw the pool transferred from the *O'Brien* to the USS *Merrill* and then on to the USS *Wainwright*. The pool transfers were accomplished by a ship-based surveillance helicopter with room for only one or two extra passengers, necessitating the prioritization of personnel, baggage, and equipment. This plan ensured that the two pool photographers (still and video) were ready to go by another helicopter to the newly discovered mine danger area and photograph the recently laid mines and their subsequent destruction. The rapidity and efficiency with which pool members were transported to the scene of the action greatly impressed the media pool, inexperienced and veterans alike.

On 16 April, the pool observed and reported on the *Samuel B. Roberts* under tow by a contract tug and escorted by the *Wainwright* after the mine strike. Good still photos and video footage were obtained, but no interviews with crew from the *Roberts* were possible at that time. Transfer of media products was accomplished in an unprecedented link-up with an NBC helicopter based in the region which hovered over the *Wainwright*'s deck, allowing same-day coverage in the United States via satellite. All concerned were impressed with the flow of information, access to fast-breaking news, and the support by the Navy. At this point in the operation, pool deactivation and return to shore appeared likely, but all members sensed that something else was in the offing.

By the morning of 17 April the pool had transferred back to the USS *Jack Williams* and the media escort officers received preliminary information about action to be taken by U.S. forces as a measured response to the Iranian mines laid in international waters, one of which was struck by the *Roberts*. On the morning of the 17th, the pool was briefed in general terms by the Commander, Destroyer Squadron 22, also aboard the *Jack Williams,* on the forthcoming operation, dubbed "Operation Praying Mantis." The media's mission was to remain aboard the *Jack Williams* to cover the operation from the scene. Pool members and escorts then conducted a reconnaissance of the ship. Good camera angles were scouted and a preliminary setup was accomplished. Pool members were obviously psyched for the coming experience, and seemed to feel that this would be the ultimate test for the media pool. It was also viewed by some pool members as a recoupment for the missed opportunity in October 1987 when the media pool was not deployed for the naval shelling of the Rashadat oil platform.

Early on 18 April, D-Day, the pool was briefed "on background" with the understanding that an official announcement from Washington would be forthcoming. Three surface action groups were formed, one each to destroy two Iranian oil platforms (which were being used to direct and coordinate

Iranian military operations in the Gulf) and one to sink the Iranian frigate *Sabalan*. The pool was with the latter group—Surface Action Group D—aboard the *Jack Williams*. This group's mission was not revealed to the media initially, as it might not be executed and would therefore remain classified for possible future action. (The mission was later divulged by the Pentagon.)

H-hour had come and gone for the Sirri and Sassan platform operations. As reports came in on those attacks, the mission of Surface Action Group D, find and sink the *Sabalan*, appeared unlikely to occur. The pool accompanying was frustrated and felt left out of the action. As the pool waited, it took special note of the other action groups' activities. Of particular interest was the dramatic audio heard over bridge-to-bridge radio of the *Wainwright*'s warning to an Iranian missile patrol boat interfering with the Sirri platform attack—"This is a warning. Stop and abandon ship. I intend to sink you." As information about the initial engagements of the platforms began to come in—first slowly, then in rapid succession—the "news" became almost overwhelming. The print and television correspondents were drafting their stories with moment-by-moment, real-time updates.

Meanwhile, Surface Action Group D had sailed into the Strait of Hormuz, with no contact or sighting of an Iranian warship to that point. As the group turned and headed back into the gulf, it received a report that the *Sabalan*'s sister ship, the *Sahand*, was moving out of port and headed toward the group with obvious hostile intent. The Commander, Joint Task Force Middle East, called the Commander, Destroyer Squadron 22, on the *Jack Williams* and passed on this elegantly simple order: "The *Sahand* is in your area. Take her." Action Group D maneuvered and awaited her arrival. U.S. Navy A-6 Intruder aircraft from the USS *Enterprise* Battle Group in the Gulf of Oman, under the control of the *Jack Williams*, flew over the *Sahand* to reconnoiter, received fire, and returned it effectively with bombs and missiles.

The USS *Joseph Strauss*, a destroyer in Action Group D, also engaged the *Sahand* with a Harpoon surface-to-surface missile. The pool soon heard that the *Sahand* lay dead in the water; it would eventually sink. This missile firing was the first action that the media pool could observe, as the *Joseph Strauss* lay just ahead. Though almost 20 miles away and out of visual range of the *Sahand*, the pool could easily hear and feel primary and secondary explosions and shock waves from the stricken enemy vessel. The pool wanted to move in on the *Sahand* wreckage and get close-ups. That was not to be.

Instead, Action Group D had to respond to reports that the *Sabalan* was steaming just south of Larak Island in the Strait of Hormuz leading toward the group. The *Sabalan*, the group's original target at the outset of the operation, fired a missile at an A-6E aircraft, which missed but prompted the A-6E to engage it with laser-guided bombs. *Sabalan* was hit and heavily damaged.

While the ongoing actions were newsworthy events for the pool, they often did not provide good visual opportunities for the still photographer and television crew. This is an age of over-the-horizon naval engagements, and the pool got a taste of what it's like to cover high-tech combat involving long-range missiles, radar intercepts, and high-altitude aircraft sorties. The visual media representatives had to be content with what they could actually see from the decks of the *Jack Williams*.

About this time the first indications of some sort of incoming missiles were noted and passed to all on board the *Jack Williams*. The call of "Silkworm inbound" could be heard loud and clear several times over the next two hours. Iranian aircraft, including a four-engine C-130 cargo aircraft possibly directing the Silkworm strikes, reportedly flew near Action Group D. The ships responded quickly and effectively. Clearly evident to the media pool were the ships' defensive maneuverings, chaff-dispensing (designed to deflect incoming missiles), and surface-to-air missile engagements by the *Jack Williams* and the other ships in the group. (Of particular interest is that the initial ship's report indicated the missiles were Silkworms; the media accounts accurately reflected what the ship had reported. The Pentagon has since stated that there is no evidence that Silkworms were fired at the action group.)

The video and still cameras and crews, with military escort, maintained a position on the O-3 level, the very highest observation platform on the ship. Lieutenant Commander Mark Van Dyke, staff public affairs officer for the Commander, Joint Task Force Middle East, remained on the bridge with the wire and TV correspondents. These locations proved to be optimal in view of the audio, visual, and command and control aspects of the operation that were readily observable. Also evident were the fear and confusion that can be expected in any hostile environment. But the crew and pool members took it in stride. All did their jobs coolly and professionally under intense pressure. Print stories were filed continuously from the *Jack Williams,* while television and still photographic products were prepared for transfer ashore at the earliest possible opportunity.

The eventful day of 18 April 1988 ended as the *Jack Williams* was directed to remain in the area to patrol, observe, and assist in the search for a Marine helicopter reported missing that evening with two crewmen aboard.[4] These two were the only U.S. casualties that day. Later, the Commander-in-Chief, U.S. Central Command, upon discovery of the wreckage, stated that there was no indication the helicopter had been hit by hostile fire. Efforts soon began to move the pool to other vessels or back ashore, pending further hard-news opportunities. The pool's experience on the *Jack Williams* had been cordial, cooperative, and unforgettable, but it was time to move on. Pool members and escorts transferred to the USS *Lynde McCormick* on the evening of 21 April. Here was an excellent opportunity to get a new perspective on other activities of 18 April, as the *Lynde McCormick* had participated in the attack on the Sassan platform. Several more stories and videotapes resulted from this short but valuable visit.

Finally ashore the evening of 22 April, pool members rested and reflected on the previous 11 days—the longest media pool deployment since its formation. Pool accomplishments during this activation included over 2000 miles traveled, ten ships embarked, six helicopter transfers, four small-boat transfers,

14 print reports, six television scripts filed, 600 minutes of videotape, 18 rolls of still film, and three ship-to-shore transfers of pool material. Pool members described the experience as "awesome." This deployment clearly demonstrated the essential value of the pool and the military's ability to coordinate challenging pool logistical requirements without significant impact upon operations or security.

A key to the success of this pool deployment was the continuing close interaction between the pool members and their military escorts. Answering questions in a timely manner and ensuring that each pool member was kept abreast of activities, even when new information was not available, helped considerably in assuring pool members that the military was looking out for their interests, both professionally and personally. Additionally, timely information and support from the public affairs staffs of the Joint Task Force Middle East, U.S. Central Command, and the Department of Defense were invaluable.

If there was any chronic problem encountered during the deployment of the pool, it was getting print reports and photographic products—video and still—off the ship in a timely manner. As has been mentioned, video and still products were flown off by civilian news helicopters for further transfer via satellite or mail to all interested media. The helicopter linkup was a practice that had not been authorized to this point, but soon became an approved and accepted means of transfer once it was successfully tried. Operational requirements precluded quick transfer of products immediately following the 18 April action, but that was understood and accepted by all media pool members. The soonest a video and still product transfer could be made was on 20 April, again by news helicopter.

Print reports from the wire reporter were filed by the standard method used since the first pool deployment—immediate precedence military message to both the Pentagon and U.S. Central Command, who in turn distributed it immediately to all media. Delays come from the fact that a ship's operational message traffic goes out by the same system. Thus when news breaks and stories are filed, generally operational messages are also going out and take priority. Again, when all was said and done, the pool members understood and accepted the system. The command/control vessel *Jack Williams*, even with so much important operational message traffic to be sent, was willing to dedicate a word processor and operator solely to media pool print reports, shortening the waiting time for reports to be typed and coded into message format. The bottom line—print reports got off the ship as soon as operationally feasible.

The end result of this whole experience for the pool was wide and accurate reporting of events as they occurred. The fog of war is always present in hostile actions, and events tend to become clear only incrementally, as more information is received from different sources, but the pool was constantly updated and accurate follow-up stories resulted. As evidence of the close pool interaction with the ship, when the *Jack Williams'* skipper expressed concern that he was unable to communicate frankly with his crew over the intercom without risk of being quoted, the pool agreed that no one would report anything the CO said over the intercom and did not want reported. This is probably unprecedented in media-military relations, at least since World War II, but reflects the compromises that often occur in order to get the job done. That it happened is a credit to the professionals in the pool.

But what about future media involvement in ground operations with Army or Marine forces? Aren't those types of media deployments very different and more difficult to control than maritime operations, where a media pool can be held incommunicado aboard a ship, with their reportage virtually hostage to the ship's captain and his mission? Yes. Certainly there are different concerns in working with media pools in different scenarios. Those must be planned for and dealt with case by case. But even in Grenada, with only frantic last-minute planning to accommodate the media, accurate coverage resulted. Most significant, however, has been the deployment of national media pools on the eight occasions previously mentioned, allowing development, testing, and refinement of procedures in supporting and controlling media pool coverage under a variety of circumstances with different types of forces.

We have now run the gamut—from a hasty, makeshift pool, organized to cover the latter part of the Grenada rescue operation; through training deployments and the activation of the DOD national media pool for the first transit of reflagged Kuwaiti tankers; to the first employment of the DOD media pool during hostile action by U.S. forces, a thoroughly planned contingency that involved public affairs from the beginning as an integral part of the operation. Regional pool activities ceased in the Gulf in July of 1988. In its place, a program of unilateral embarkations began to accommodate the many requests received from news organizations asking for the opportunity to send representatives to ships in the Persian Gulf. Of course, the Department of Defense and U.S. Central Command retain the option of reactivating the pool, should that become necessary.

The military's planning, coordination, and execution of the media pool deployments to cover operations in the Persian Gulf and elsewhere have set the standard for future media pool operations. The evolution of pool deployments to cover both ground-based force deployments during training and contingency operations and sea-based deployments in the Persian Gulf involving all services has clearly addressed the Sidle Panel's statement of principle—"U.S. news media [should] cover U.S. military operations to the maximum degree possible consistent with mission security and the safety of U.S. forces."[5]

The procedure is not perfect. We can always improve. Few military plans ever work exactly as they are designed to work. They inevitably require modifications based on changing circumstances and the needs of the participants, and constant review. That is happening now at all levels within the military. Every media pool deployment in the Persian Gulf—35 in all— provided some new perspective on military-media relations. But the proof is in the execution. It has worked for routine deployments and for hostilities experienced thus far. The media pool has come of age and military-media relations are as good as they have been since World War II. There is no reason why they can't get even better.

Notes

1. For excellent background on military-media relations, particularly those during the Grenada operation, see Peter Braestrup, "Background Paper," in *Battle Lines: Report of the Twentieth Century Fund Task Force on the Military and the Media* (New York: Priority Press, 1985), pp. 19–160.

2. Tim Ahern, "White Smoke in the Persian Gulf," *Washington Journalism Review*, 9 (October 1987), 18.

3. Mark Thompson, "With the Press Pool in the Persian Gulf," *Columbia Journalism Review* (November/December 1987), 46.

4. For an interesting perspective on the events surrounding 18 April 1988 by pool member Richard Pyle of the Associated Press, see his "Covering a Mini-War: Sometimes the Pool Works," *Washington Journalism Review*, 10 (July/August 1988), 14–17.

5. *Battle Lines*, p. 165.

This article appeared originally in the March 1989 issue of *Parameters*.

........8

The Panama Press Pool Deployment: A Critique.........

By Fred S. Hoffman

Excessive concern for secrecy prevented the Defense Department's media pool from reporting the critical opening actions of Operation Just Cause, the U.S. invasion of Panama on 20 December 1989. Because of a secrecy-driven decision by Secretary of Defense Richard B. Cheney, the pool was called out too late and arrived too late to cover the decisive U.S. assaults in that brief war. Military leaders played NO part in shaping that decision. Mr. Cheney said his first priority was safeguarding the security of the operation and that he "was aware of the conflict" between that imperative and the goal of getting the pool to Panama in time. As Mr. Cheney's public affairs adviser, Assistant Secretary of Defense for Public Affairs Pete Williams should have foreseen the consequences of a late pool deployment. He should have tried to convince Mr. Cheney that the pool had to be launched early enough to reach Panama before the operation kicked off.

Over the five-year history of Pentagon-sponsored pools, including a year-long series in the Persian Gulf, hundreds of newsmen and newswomen demonstrated that they could be trusted to respect essential ground rules, including operational security. Unless the Defense Department's leaders are prepared to extend that trust in hot-war situations, the pool probably will be of little value.

Excessive concern for secrecy prevented timely detailed planning for the pool's coverage of Operation Just Cause. A lack of helicopters—which could have been avoided with proper planning—prevented the pool from reporting much of what was left of the action by the time the pool reached Panama. Some U.S. military concern in Panama for the safety of the pool members impeded coverage. This concern, while understandable, should *not* have been allowed to limit the pool's reporting opportunities. Newsmen and women cover wars at their own risk. The result of all this was that the 16-member pool produced stories and pictures of essentially secondary value.

Southern Command Public Affairs Officers (PAOs) had little success in getting the pool to any remaining newsworthy action in the mop-up of the already-defeated Panama Defense Force and ragtag Dignity Battalion holdouts. PAOs tried to find "story ideas," as one of them put it, but too many of these turned out to be disappointments or dry holes.

Overall, there were important instances of less than effective leadership and performance in the Office of the Assistant Secretary of Defense for Public Affairs and among some of the senior PAOs in Panama: lapses in staff work, flawed procedures, and problems in organization. Southern Command PAOs failed to provide regular operational briefings for the pool to keep it informed of developments all through Panama. There was only one such briefing, more than 24 hours into the pool's four-day deployment. Malfunctioning fax equipment and understaffing at the Pentagon, plus communications problems at the Southern Command Media Center in Panama, caused serious delays in getting out print pool reports and still photos.

The decision to send a news pool from Washington was highly questionable. The story could have—and, in my opinion, should have—been covered by a pool formed from U.S. news personnel already in Panama. Such a pool could have been put in place before American forces attacked. It could have had a front-row view of the assault on Noriega's main headquarters, the Comandancia, a short distance down the hill from Southern Command headquarters on Quarry Heights. Some locally based U.S. news personnel could have been pre-positioned to cover attacks on other key objectives as well. Colonel Ron Sconyers, then the Southern Command's Public Affairs Officer, suggested to Mr. Williams that the story could be covered by a pool drawn from American news personnel already in Panama—personnel with whom he had worked. Sconyers had mustered such a pool many times before on smaller operations without any security breach.

It should be noted here that the Pentagon pool was established to enable U.S. news personnel to report the earliest possible action in a U.S. military operation *in a remote area where there was no other American press presence.* Panama did not fit that description. But Williams, following discussions with Cheney, sent the national pool from Washington. It appears that a key reason for this decision was what Cheney later described in an interview as a "desire to avoid being criticized for not using" the pool in the Panama situation. As it turned out, the Pentagon pool landed in Panama about four hours after U.S. troops launched their attacks on key targets. Even then, whatever helicopter lift Southern Command PAOs could round up was swiftly snatched away for higher-priority operational purposes. Ground transportation was deemed too risky because of sniping. Also, the Bridge of the Americas which spans the Panama Canal was closed for hours on the first day of the operation. The helicopter situation eased after about 36 hours, but the story was rapidly winding down by that time.

From the outset, the members of the pool met one frustration after another. PAOs in Panama unwittingly fed the pool's justified irritation by hauling its members to some "events" that had nothing to do with the fighting they so badly wanted to see and report. As a result, there were suggestions that the pool was being manipulated to serve the Bush Administration's political and diplomatic interests. So far as I could determine, there was no effort to manipulate the pool in Panama. Rather, it was a matter of maladroitness, sometimes good intentions gone awry, and unanticipated obstacles. Some examples:

Late that exhausting first day, the pool was taken to meet the arriving U.S. ambassador for a news conference. One pooler described this happening as "worthless." Asked why it was done, an escort officer explained that there was nothing else going on at the time and that it was a matter of poolers "either doing that or hanging around the press center." This was especially irksome to the pool because its members had been exposed, shortly after landing in Panama, to a briefing by John Bushnell, U.S. Embassy Chargé d'Affaires. A reporter who was there described it as a lecture on the history of Panama. What the pool apparently didn't know was that Mr. Bushnell was a last-minute stand-in. The Southern Command PAOs had expected the star of the event to be the newly-sworn-in Panamanian President Endara making his first appearance before the press. But Endara refused to do this at an American base. So the intended "exclusive" bombed, and Bushnell was drafted in Endara's place.

Sometimes the pool was diverted from a promising objective because escort officers discovered, belatedly, the presence of Special Operations soldiers. Such troops are under standing orders to shun the press. More than once, the pool encountered unit commanders who had no idea what the pool was all about and felt they had to check up the chain of command. Obviously, word about the pool and its mission had not reached down through the military echelons, as should have been assured by senior PAOs of Southern Command and the 18th Airborne Corps, which did the fighting.

I could find no evidence—except for standing orders governing Special Operations troops, including the Rangers—that any senior civilian official or military commander had issued written or verbal instructions to refuse interviews or other contact with news personnel. The restrictions on the Rangers were eased on the second day of the operation.

One senior PAO did advise Major General James Johnson, commander of the 82nd Airborne Division, not to talk with newsmen. General Johnson accepted this advice from Lieutenant Colonel Ned Longsworth, who said he had received guidance to that effect. But when asked about this, Longsworth said he could not recall who gave him such guidance. This remains a mystery.

In my discussion with the top generals involved in Operation Just Cause I heard only expressions of support for the pool concept and regret that it didn't work as it should have in Panama. Skeptics may regard these expressions as tinged with after-the-fact wisdom, but I believe they can be viewed as hopeful indicators for the future. General Max Thurman, the head of Southern Command, said, "I think we made a mistake by not having some of the press pool in with the 18th Airborne Corps so they could move with the troops." Army Lieutenant General Carl W. Stiner, who commanded all the combat troops in the invasion, said he could have received a smaller pool at Ft. Bragg, N.C., and taken it with him to Panama ahead of the paratroop deployment. It could have been briefed, sequestered, and positioned to witness the opening of the attack, said Stiner, who flew to Panama on Monday, 18 December. The assaults began early 20 December. General Stiner's scenario would have required a much earlier callout of the pool. It actually was mustered the evening of Tuesday, 19 December. In fact the pool question still was being discussed in the White House Oval Office as late as Tuesday afternoon and a "go" order wasn't given by Williams to his staff and the Southern Command PAO until about 5:00 P.M. that day for a 7:30 P.M. callout—only five and one half hours before H-hour.

Major General William A. Roosma suggested that, in the future, the Pentagon media pool members should exercise several times a year with airborne troops in conjunction with periodic Emergency Development Readiness Exercises. In that way "they become part of the team" and gain experience, said Roosma, who was General Stiner's deputy commander of the 18th Airborne Corps. More frequent pool exercises—the pool was called out only once last year prior to the Panama deployment—might well serve to implant necessary ground rules and prescribed procedures more deeply in the minds of pool members and their bureau chiefs, particularly those new to pool duty. Periodic pool exercises with various elements of the armed forces, especially those with quick-reaction missions, would help accustom line outfits to contact with news people.

There was a breach of operational security rules by staff members of *Time* magazine's Washington bureau reached at a Christmas party during the Panama pool callout on the evening of 19 December, only a few hours before the pool was due to take off from Andrews Air Force Base, Maryland. This breach resulted from an open discussion at the party about who would go for *Time*—an assignment that should have been established by the bureau chief in advance. As *Time* bureau chief Stanley Cloud acknowledged: "More people knew than should have known." But that secrecy rule violation likely could have been avoided if the *Time* bureau chief had been notified at his office during daytime business hours—something made impossible because of the high-level Pentagon decision to delay the callout until after the evening news broadcasts on TV. So far as I could determine, the *Time* violation did not compromise the operation.

Some of the key problems that eventually burdened the pool had their genesis in overstress on secrecy and subsequent fumbles at the Pentagon and Southern Command in November. As a consequence, about a month of possible planning time was lost, and when Operation Just Cause was mounted there was no public affairs plan.

On 13 November, the Joint Staff sent a Top Secret warning order to Southern Command and other commands, signaling readiness for possible operations against Panama. In that message, the Joint Staff asked Southern Command to submit a public affairs plan and directed Southern Command to "be prepared to accept a media pool." On 22 November, the Southern Command Public Affairs Office sent a Top Secret fax to the Pentagon public affairs plans office. That fax was far short of a fully fleshed-out plan. It provided bare-bones public affairs guidance. Lieutenant Commander Gregory Hartung, a plans officer, took the fax message to his boss, Colonel Peter Alexandrakos. Alexandrakos prepared a Top Secret memorandum and began the process of coordinating the proposed guidance among relevant offices. As is customary, Alexandrakos invited comments.

That same day, 22 November, Hartung was summoned to the Pentagon's Inter-American Affairs Office. Hartung said he was informed by a staff officer there that then Deputy Assistant Secretary of Defense Richard C. Brown "had discussed this document at an inter-agency meeting . . . and that they decided because this scenario was so inflammatory that it should be held 'close hold' at the Office of the Assistant Secretary of Defense for Public Affairs until such time that it became necessary to have such guidance and then staffed at that time." According to Hartung's recollection, he was told to "stick it in the safe and forget about it."

In an interview, Mr. Brown said the proposed guidance document "was dynamite. . . . It really told about the mission. Given that it could be leaked, there was concern about possible compromise." One of Brown's top aides said the security concern centered on the way the document was being circulated for coordination. This aide said that the Inter-American Affairs Office "never told Public Affairs to stop what they were doing." He added: "They were advised, however, to do it in the proper channels."

Although there are differing versions of what advice Hartung was given, the result was that the message was put into a safe and effectively buried there. While the document failed to meet the requirement for a complete public affairs plan, it should have served to alert staff officers that follow-through action was imperative. Four Public Affairs staff officers, three of them at the Pentagon and one at Southern Command, failed to follow through—failed to question why nothing was being done to fulfill the Joint Staff's requirement for a public affairs plan for what turned out to be Operation Just Cause. The

Inter-American Affairs objections were never brought to the attention of Williams, as should have happened. This demonstrates a weakness in the planning system. It needs closer oversight in the front office of the Assistant Secretary of Defense for Public Affairs.

If the normal planning process had been carried out, it is quite likely that some of the problems which cropped up for the pool during Operation Just Cause would have been anticipated. A careful plan would have provided for earmarking helicopters to move the pool, for dedicating aircraft to carry photographic and other pool products to the United States, and for adequate communications facilities to accommodate not only the pool, but the hundreds of other reporters and photographers who flooded into the country. Southern Command did have a contingency plan for accommodating the pool, but its provisions were very general. What was needed was a specific plan tailored to the upcoming operation.

As Major General Roosma said, "A public affairs annex to an operational plan must be written in great detail. . . . The time to prepare such a plan is not during great crisis, but beforehand."

The first discussion of a possible pool to cover Operation Just Cause came on Sunday, 17 December, in a meeting at which President Bush presided in his study. This was the meeting that produced the decision to send American troops into Panama. Mr. Cheney said the Department of Defense pool would be activated to go in with the initial forces, according to White House spokesman Marlin Fitzwater, who was present. Bush asked whether the pool would come from Washington or would be organized in Panama. The President was told it would come from Washington, Fitzwater said. Bush indicated concern as to whether this could be done while still protecting operational security.

The issue came up again at the White House on Tuesday afternoon, ten hours or so before the operation was due to start. Vice President Quayle asked if the pool couldn't be organized in Panama rather than being dispatched from Washington, Fitzwater said, adding: "No one had a good answer as to why it had to come from Washington." According to this account, President Bush and Vice President Quayle remained skeptical that the pool would be able to maintain secrecy. In the final analysis, Fitzwater said, the President "left it up" to Cheney.

Meanwhile, on Monday morning Williams said he was called to Cheney's office and told that the President had decided to proceed with an operation against Noriega and that a pool would be used to cover it. "You can't mention this to anybody," Williams quoted Cheney as telling him. Williams said he had several conversations with Cheney on Monday and Tuesday. "There was never any doubt in anyone's mind that there was going to be a pool," Williams said.

However, the issue of whether it would be a pool drawn from news people already in Panama or the national media pool in Washington appears to have been a live one until late Tuesday afternoon. "The Secretary and I talked about whether to use a national or regional pool," Williams recalled. In the end, he said, "We decided to use the national pool because we were confident operational security could be preserved, we were accustomed to it, and we had used a pool" the previous May (in connection with a troop reinforcement to Panama). Another reason for this decision, Williams said, was a belief that the Washington-based pool members "knew the ground rules."

Cheney mentioned somewhat different reasons for opting to send the pool from Washington—a decision that the Defense Secretary said was in accord with Mr. Williams' recommendation. "The pool was created for this kind of situation," said Cheney. On this, he was misinformed. As mentioned earlier, the pool was organized as a vehicle to provide U.S. news personnel early access to fighting by American forces in *remote* areas—not a Panama with a resident U.S. press corps and an existing American base structure.

This illustrates how the perception of the pool's purpose has become skewed since it was established in the wake of the Pentagon's ill-advised denial of access for news reporting during U.S. military actions on the Caribbean island of Grenada in 1983. Cheney also said that he had a "sense of special loyalty to people who cover the Pentagon," and that "it was important that there be that kind of coverage." Actually, the news pool that flew to Panama included only one Pentagon regular, NBC's Fred Francis.

As for the timing of the pool callout—the most critical factor in the outcome of its deployment—Cheney said his decision was conditioned by an overriding need to maintain the "maximum security possible to avoid compromising the operation and to preserve the element of surprise." Despite the attempt to keep a secrecy lid firmly in place, reports were appearing on TV and on the news wires Tuesday depicting unusual military activity at bases in the United States and Panama. Alluding to these reports, Cheney said, "We were very concerned about the situation—that the Panama Defense Force might be waiting for us." So, Cheney said, "We basically decided to notify the pool after the evening news Tuesday to minimize the possibility of leaks."

The 7:30 P.M. callout guaranteed that the pool would reach Panama hours after the operation began just before 1:00 A.M. Wednesday, the 20th of December. Cheney said, "I did it with full knowledge" of what his decision would mean for the pool. The Pentagon chief made it clear it was basically his decision, but Williams obviously was in full agreement. "We decided 7:30 P.M. was a good time to call it out," Williams said. "I never suggested an earlier callout," he said when asked about this.

General Colin Powell, Chairman of the Joint Chiefs of Staff, recalling the White House discussion about the pool on Tuesday, said, "The final judgment was made in the Oval Office and that was that we ought to have a pool." Did General Powell make any recommendations to Cheney or Williams on how and when the pool should be called out? The four-star general said he was "left out of the pattern" in this regard, that he discussed the pool with Cheney "in only the most general terms," and that "I left it up to Pete Williams." Lieutenant General Tom Kelly, the Joint Staff Director of Operations, said, "We didn't play any role" in the framing of the civilian decisions on the pool callout. Williams said he didn't hear from senior military leaders on the question of the timing of the pool deployment.

Bound by a secrecy rule laid down by Cheney, Williams informed only two members of his staff on Monday, 18 December, of the upcoming operation and the likelihood of a news pool being formed to cover it. These two were Deputy Assistant Secretary Bob Taylor and Major John Smith, Williams' military assistant. It wasn't until the next morning that Williams brought his own planning staff into the process and several hours after that on Tuesday that Williams began discussions with Southern Command PAO Colonel Ron Sconyers about a probable pool. Therefore, more than 24 hours of immediate planning time was lost.

Taylor was set to work gathering information to refresh Williams' knowledge of pool call-up procedures and similar matters. Smith, who had served in Southern Command, provided information on the public affairs setup down there. There was some "brainstorming," as Smith described it, but apparently no detailed planning on that Monday.

The only conversation outside the small circle of knowledgeable persons in Williams' office came about midday on Monday. It was initiated by mid-level officers from the Joint Staff who wanted to discuss possible airlift arrangements for a media pool deployment. These discussions were inconclusive because options offered from the Joint Staff would have landed the pool in Panama about 12 hours after the attacks opened. Even after Williams brought in his planning staff to start detailed preparations on Tuesday, debate over whether to use a Panama-based pool or send one from Washington lingered into the afternoon. The discussion became moot after the White House meeting, and Williams called Sconyers at about 5:00 P.M. to inform him that the national media pool would be heading his way that night.

To have made the pool deployment a success, a firm decision on sending it should have been made, if not on Monday, by Tuesday morning. The pool could have been called out about midday Tuesday and flown to Panama to arrive by early evening—in plenty of time to be sequestered, briefed, and pre-positioned near possible objectives to witness the major attacks.

In Panama, chief PAO Sconyers received some indications on Monday, 18 December, that there might be a military operation against Noriega, but this was not confirmed for him until Tuesday morning when an operations officer gave him a detailed briefing including specific objectives. Colonel Sconyers said he was told he could not share that information with anybody. These security restraints, he said, barred him from starting preparations. At that time, he said, he was thinking in terms of using a locally based pool and this conditioned some of his moves. As of Tuesday morning, he said he considered asking for specific assignment of helicopters to support the pool, but he didn't feel at that time that he would need them for the Panama-based pool. He intended to place that pool to observe the fighting below Quarry Heights and possibly at Ft.

Amador. After he was notified officially at 5:00 P.M. Tuesday that the national media pool would be coming from Washington, Sconyers said he asked for helicopter support. By this time, virtually all the helicopters were assigned to carry combat troops.

Looking back, General Thurman said he might have been able to reach out and place possibly two helicopters at the disposal of the pool if he had known on Monday that it was coming from Washington. Sconyers did manage to get a small UH-1 helicopter for the pool. But a Huey holds only eight. So he asked for a larger one, and a CH-47 was eventually provided, only to be taken away Wednesday morning after ferrying the newsmen and newswomen from Howard AFB to Ft. Clayton, where the pool got to watch TV broadcasts of President Bush's speech and a Pentagon news conference by Secretary Cheney and General Powell.

Although Sconyers did not have definite word on Monday that an operation against Noriega was in the offing, he was reading signs and probably should have anticipated the need for helicopters to move a pool, even if that pool was organized in Panama. In his long-term planning, Sconyers and his staff had arranged for filing facilities at a media center on Quarry Heights, but these were designed to serve a limited pool, not the horde of newsmen who flooded in starting the day after the pool reached Panama.

In any event, those media center filing facilities, particularly telephone lines, proved to be inadequate even for the pool and were overwhelmed when the larger number of reporters converged on that center. Sconyers also underestimated a need for more people to handle the big influx of newsmen. He was offered additional help early on, but declined at the time. The upshot was that he found himself spending much of his time and energies in arranging billeting, feeding, and other necessary services for hundreds of news people. To that extent, he was diverted from serving the pool.

Back in Washington, Colonel Alexandrakos, head of Williams' Plans division, and some of his staff began the callout as ordered at about 7:30 P.M. Tuesday. Pool members were supposed to report to Andrews AFB by 9:30 P.M. for a planned departure at 11 P.M. Immediately, the Plans officers manning the phones ran into difficulties in getting the word to some of the news people on the pool roster. Some of this difficulty could be attributed to the fact that the callout came during the week before Christmas when there were news staff parties and there were news people on vacation.

The situation wasn't helped by apparent confusion in the callout process at the Pentagon. Alexandrakos said he was ordered by Deputy Assistant Secretary Taylor in mid-callout to expand the pool by going back to all the wire services and inviting each to send a reporter and a photographer. Taylor said in an interview Alexandrakos apparently had not understood that there were supposed to be slots on the pool for two representatives of each of the three wire services. That decision was made earlier on Tuesday, Taylor said.

The pool already had been expanded in an unprecedented way when Williams offered NBC the opportunity to bring along on the flight to Panama a satellite uplink dish which, together with its associated equipment, weighed more than a ton. NBC arranged for that satellite dish and two technicians with an outside company which provides such services. In effect, this add-on widened the radius of knowledge outside the normal pool. It created the potential for a security breach by technicians who never had been involved in pool activities and never had been subjected to the discipline of operational security ground rules. The satellite uplink, however, did help the NBC correspondent, Fred Francis, in beaming his broadcasts from Panama. There is no evidence that the addition of the technicians led to any security compromise.

As another by-product of the confusion which surrounded the callout, the primary pooler for one newspaper and his alternate both showed up at Andrews. The alternate, who did not make the trip, then called home. Normally this would be a violation of a ground rule, but an escorting officer gave permission for the call.

Apart from the incident at the *Time* magazine Christmas party, there was another report of a security breach allegedly involving the pool. This report reached President Bush from House Speaker Tom Foley during their conversation about seven hours before the attacks opened. It did not check out. A top aide to the Speaker said he is convinced a newsman's probing call to Foley was prompted by reports on TV and news wires of military movements around bases in the United States and Panama, not by any leak from the pool. This view is supported by the fact that the President told associates he spoke with Foley at about 6:00 P.M. Tuesday, which was one and one-half hours before the callout began.

Most of the poolers arrived at Andrews properly equipped. One lacked a passport. One lacked a shot record. Alexandrakos decided neither document was needed because the pool was going to be operating on and from U.S. bases in Panama. Dick Thompson, *Time* magazine correspondent, had to rush from the Christmas party, so he didn't have a chance to change clothes or to pick up his writing tools. He went to tropical Panama in a winter suit. The pool left Andrews at 11:26 P.M. and was informed, when airborne, where they were going and why. Most already suspected their destination was Panama.

Shortly after the pool landed at Howard AFB in Panama at 5:00 A.M. Wednesday it became clear that it wasn't going to spring into action. A CH-47 helicopter arrived about one-half hour later, and it took still another half hour to load it up with the cumbersome satellite uplink dish and other equipment.

Sconyers had planned to run the pool up to Quarry Heights by road, but the closure of the Bridge of the Americas across the canal and reports that Quarry Heights was under fire impelled a change in plan. Instead, the pool was taken to Ft. Clayton, about ten minutes away by helicopter. This is when things all began to go downhill as it dawned on the reporters that they were not moving to the scene of combat. By 7:00 A.M., it was becoming clear at the Pentagon that the pool was immobilized. Taylor and Williams urged Sconyers in succeeding hours to get the pool to the action. At no time, however, did Williams contact General Powell, the Joint Chiefs of Staff Chairman, for help in this situation. He should have done so as soon as he became aware of the problem. Powell heard nothing about the pool's plight until Thursday afternoon, about 30 hours later. "I thought everything went smoothly," Powell said. He said he "didn't have a single clue" the pool was bogged down until newsmen informed him. Powell indicated he would have been prepared to act promptly if he had heard from Williams. "Once it became clear that things were not going well, it should have been worked through command channels," the JCS Chairman said. "It never became a matter of discussion for me and General Thurman."

When the pool finally did get moving, Alexandrakos and Sconyers kept it in a single unit rather than splitting it to cover more of the story. Alexandrakos said the pool was kept together because of transportation limitations. It was split into two sections on the second day of the operation. The first time the pool had a chance to get anywhere near any shooting was around 10:00 A.M., when Sconyers managed to get a helicopter back and the group was flown to Ft. Amador, across the bay from Quarry Heights and the main part of Panama City.

Here is the way that Ken Merida of the *Dallas Morning News* described what the pool found there: "Even at Ft. Amador, a military installation shared by the United States and Panama under the Panama Canal Treaties, the action was largely over. U.S. troops had repeatedly shelled the barracks of the Panamanian Defense Forces in the early morning hours when we were still on a military transport plane. All that was left to do was smoke out a few remaining Noriega loyalists, none of whom surrendered in our presence."

While at Ft. Amador, the poolers could see smoke rising from around the battered remains of the Commandancia in Panama City several miles away. "We were told that because of continued sniper fire on the first day it was too dangerous for us to visit the neighborhood of Chorillo which housed another of Noriega's headquarters and was still burning from heavy shelling by U.S. troops," Merida said. "It was also too dangerous, we were told, to take a helicopter tour of Panama City."

This issue of the pool's safety was a sore one. Some members of the pool felt it was being used as an excuse by escorts to divert the news people from hot military action. Lieutenant Colonel Ned Longsworth, who was chief escort for the pool at Ft. Amador, acknowledged that he "may have been a little too protective at Ft. Amador." Longsworth claimed that, otherwise, safety was not invoked to prevent moving the pool to newsworthy sites. But Kathy Lewis, reporter for the *Houston Post,* said, "We were often told we could NOT go to a certain area because of concern about snipers or other threats to our safety."

As for the rejection of poolers' requests to be flown over the city, Longsworth said, "I wasn't going to put a helicopter pilot's life on the line to fly over the city when there still was fire." Regardless, Longsworth said, "The pilots advised that they didn't want to fly over Panama City. They were still catching rounds. This was not for the safety of the pool. The pilots thought it would endanger their ship." I strongly doubt that any news professional would expect members of the armed forces to risk their lives just for the purpose of getting reporters and photographers a story. But concern for safety of news people should never be used by the military as an excuse to seal them off from the scene of fighting.

After-action reports prepared by members of the pool and interviews point up a number of other episodes which were especially galling to them. Photographers and reporters were incensed when they were told they could not interview or take pictures of American wounded. This bar was ordered by Williams' office out of concern that pictures or identification of wounded might appear on TV or in print before next-of-kin were notified officially. In this case I feel the bar was proper because it avoided the possibility of causing shock and pain to relatives who might not yet have been informed. Later in the week, after notification of families was assured, wounded were televised at a military hospital in San Antonio, Texas.

Another frustration involving casualties is inexplicable. In a meeting on the first night in Panama, pool photographers were turned aside by Colonel Sconyers when they sought to photograph caskets bearing men killed in action. The question of notification of next-of-kin did not apply in this case because the caskets were closed and bore no identification of the bodies inside. Two pool photographers and a military escort quoted Sconyers as saying the caskets would be sent to the United States later in the week. The caskets showed up at Dover AFB in Delaware well before that time. When asked about this, Sconyers said he did not remember any discussions with members of the pool about the caskets, but he conceded later that he may have had such an exchange with poolers. He noted things were in a pretty hectic state at that time.

Members of the pool were indignant when they were denied access to a place where Panamanian prisoners were being held. As Longsworth explained it, a younger officer in charge refused to allow the pool to enter the prisoner detention area until he checked with his commander. Longsworth said he contacted Southern Command headquarters and finally received permission for the pool to take pictures of the detainees.

Still another confrontation between escort and pool occurred when Longsworth told photographers they could not photograph damaged helicopters at Howard AFB. Here, Longsworth said he was carrying out an order by Air Force Brigadier General Robin Tarnow, commander of the 830th Air Division, who was concerned that photographers might inadvertently take pictures of classified equipment on the field at the time. Longsworth should have interceded for the photographers. Experience has shown, notably in the Persian Gulf, that photographers will refrain from picturing sensitive equipment if asked. It seems that such an agreement could have been reached with the photographers in this case, thus allowing them to take pictures of non-sensitive damaged helicopters.

Members of the pool resented what they regarded as special treatment accorded to ABC personality Sam Donaldson, who arrived with an entourage the day after the main attacks. "When Sam Donaldson arrived, it was like the President had walked into the media center," said one military escort who shared the pool's feeling of resentment. This officer said Sconyers was "given over basically to supporting Sam Donaldson."

Sconyers and his deputy, Lieutenant Colonel Bob Donnelly, made it clear they were unhappy at what they hinted was pressure from Washington to give Donaldson favored treatment. It is self-evident that there should never be any special treatment or favoritism for any outside news personnel at the expense of the pool.

"It was a nightmare," said Army Captain Barbara Summers. "The faxing and refaxing operation was a nightmare," said the *Houston Post*'s Kathy Lewis. Both were describing their experiences, thousands of miles apart, in trying to get written pool reports from Panama to the Pentagon for distribution. Summers was part of an undermanned crew at the Pentagon, grappling with a faulty fax machine and torturous telephone communications. Lewis was a reporter serving with the media pool in Panama, harried by the same problems.

While TV and radio newsmen with the pool transmitted their reports without major difficulty, the newspaper, wire service, and magazine reporters and still photographers ran into obstacle after obstacle. The first obstacle arose Wednesday morning when the initial writing pool report was filed in Panama to the Pentagon. The fax machine in the Plans office was broken. As a result of this malfunction, the machine was cutting copy short at the margins. Sergeant Rheuben Douthitt located a replacement, but then he and other staff members had difficulty reading the incoming material. The Pentagon staffers then tried to phone the media center at Quarry Heights in Panama to clarify the copy. However, sometimes the calls were misdirected by the Quarry Heights switchboard and sometimes the phones in the media center went unanswered. It took as long as two hours to get a call through. By this time, bureau chiefs from news organizations represented on the pool were calling the Pentagon demanding to know why they weren't getting the pool reports from the scene.

"Hours after the fact we discovered there had been transmission problems with our morning reports, and hours after the late afternoon ones were sent we learned the fax machines were cutting off large margins," Kathy Lewis said. "We had to resend all of our dispatches," said Thompson of *Time*.

Facing these obstructions, reporters asked Colonel Alexandrakos for permission to depart from normal pool rules and dictate their reports by telephone to one of the wire services as a means of speeding up the distribution. Members of the pool said that Alexandrakos refused permission until he could check with Washington. That caused further delay. Bob Kearns of Reuters and Steven Komarow of the Associated Press took matters into their own hands and dictated by phone directly to their wire services.

Pool photographers suffered through painfully slow and frequently interrupted picture transmission by telephone line from Panama. "The first day or two the phone line situation was next to impossible," said Tim Aubry, Reuters photographer. As Aubry and UPI photographer Matt Mendelshon explained it, operators in Panama kept checking the phone lines periodically during transmission of pictures. This caused a "hit" on the line resulting in the appearance of a black line across the picture. Therefore, the pictures had to be resent whenever this happened. Aubry estimated it took about ten hours to send six to eight photos. It should have taken about ten minutes a picture.

Sconyers and his staff had arranged for only enough telephone lines to accommodate the pool. Once other news personnel began pouring into the media center Thursday night, the pool had to scramble for lines. "With the new arrivals, the task of securing a phone line out was nearly impossible," Aubry said. "It took up to an hour at times waiting for a phone line out to file our pictures."

Pool photographers complained that film material that was supposed to have been flown to the United States either arrived very late or not at all. "There were no arrangements or priority given to the idea of transporting material out of Panama to Washington or New York," said Aubry. "The first pool material shipped out on Thursday, including raw transparency film, service negatives, and clear negative film, did not arrive at its destination until Saturday."

Cynthia Johnson, *Time* photographer, told this story: "Arrangements were supposedly made to send my Wednesday film out on a military aircraft headed for Dover Air Force Base (Delaware) on Thursday. We had a courier in place to transport the film to our lab when it arrived. The plane arrived, but the film wasn't on it. After much phoning back and forth in the middle of the night, my film was discovered in someone's in-box at Howard Air Force Base." Sconyers should have anticipated a need for dedicated aircraft as a backup in the event that primary transmission means failed. Instead, the only arrangement made was to try to send pool materials back to the States on planes already scheduled to carry cargo or passengers.

The problems back at the Pentagon in handling the print pool reports were aggravated by the fact that most of the small staff left behind by Alexandrakos was inexperienced in pool matters. Although Alexandrakos knew Tuesday morning that the media pool might be sent to Panama, he failed to make sure that each of his staff knew what they were supposed to do when the copy began rolling in from Panama. To have prepared his staff properly over the long term, Alexandrakos should have assigned specific tasks to each member and exercised the team periodically.

Marine Major Shelley Rogers and Captain Summers improvised. They organized themselves and two enlisted men into teams of two each so there would be around-the-clock coverage. This meant 12-hour shifts. Rogers had additional responsibilities—she had to work in the Pentagon's Crisis Coordination Center handling messages and other tasks. So she had to spread herself thin and this added to the burden on the other three.

Sergeant Douthitt was the only member of this small team who had experience with the pool. When he became aware Tuesday evening of what was about to happen, he pulled out a binder containing standard operating procedures developed in the past and gave it to Major Rogers. But it was too close to the event for a simple reading of the SOP to prepare sufficiently anybody who had not previously handled such responsibilities. Examination of the SOP shows a total lack of any provisions for Pentagon handling of pool products other than print reports.

Apparently there has never been a requirement laid down by the Pentagon that organizations participating in the still photo activities of a pool must share their products with photo agencies outside the pool. This is a loophole which must be closed. The pool must serve the entire news industry.

As long as the pool is an officially sponsored mechanism, the Defense Department must be prepared to make it work right. Accordingly, I offer the following 17 recommendations:

1. The Secretary of Defense should issue a policy directive, to be circulated throughout the Department and the Armed Services, stating explicitly his official sponsorship of the media pool and requiring full support for it. That policy statement should make it clear to all that the pool *must* be given every assistance to report combat by U.S. troops from the start of operations.

2. All operational plans drafted by the Joint Staff must have an annex spelling out measures to assure that the pool will move with the lead elements of U.S. forces and cover the earliest stages of operations. This principle should be incorporated in overall public affairs plans.

3. A Deputy Assistant Secretary of Defense for Public Affairs should closely monitor development of operation-related public affairs plans to assure they fulfill all requirements for pool coverage. The Assistant Secretary of Defense for Public Affairs (ASD-PA) should review all such plans. In advance of military action, those plans should be briefed to the Secretary of Defense and the Chairman of the Joint Chiefs of Staff along with the operation plans.

Public affairs staff officers and key staff personnel representing policy offices, such as International Security Affairs, should be brought into the planning process at the very earliest stage. The practice of keeping key staff officers with high security clearances out of the planning process in order to limit access to sensitive information should be followed only sparingly and eliminated where possible.

4. In the run-up to a military operation, the Chairman of the Joint Chiefs of Staff should send out a message ordering all commanders to give full cooperation to the media pool and its escorts. This requirement should be spelled out unambiguously and should reach down through all the echelons in the chain of command. Such a message should make clear that necessary resources, such as helicopters, ground vehicles, communications equipment, etc., must be earmarked specifically for pool use, that the pool *must* have ready

access to the earliest action, and that the safety of the pool members must not be used as a reason to keep the pool from the action.

5. The ASD-PA must be prepared to weigh in aggressively with the Secretary of Defense and the JCS Chairman where necessary to overcome any secrecy or other obstacles blocking prompt deployment of a pool to the scene of action.

6. After a pool has been deployed the ASD-PA must be kept informed in a timely fashion of any hitches that may arise. He must be prepared to act immediately, to contact the JCS Chairman, the Joint Staff Director of Operations, and other senior officers who can serve to break through any obstacles to the pool. The ASD-PA should call on the Defense Secretary for help as needed.

7. The ASD-PA should study a proposal by several of the Panama poolers that future pools deploy in two sections. The first section would be very small and would include only reporters and photographers. The second section, coming later, would bring in supporting gear, such as satellite uplink equipment.

8. The national media pool should never again be herded as a single unwieldy unit. It should be broken up after arriving at the scene of action to cover a wider spectrum of the story and then be reassembled periodically to share the reporting results.

9. The pool should be exercised at least once during each quarterly rotation with airborne and other types of military units most likely to be sent on emergency combat missions.

10. During deployments, there should be regular briefings for pool news people by senior operations officers so the poolers will have an up-to-date and complete overview of the progress of an operation they are covering.

11. There is an urgent need for restructuring of the organization which has the responsibility for handling pool reports sent to the Pentagon for processing and distribution. The ASD-PA must assure that there is adequate staffing and enough essential equipment to handle the task. The Director of Plans, so long as he has this responsibility, should clearly assign contingency duties among his staff to ensure timely handling of reports from the pool. Staffers from the Administration Office, Community Relations, and other divisions of Office of the ASD-PA should be mobilized to help in such a task as needed.

12. The ASD-PA should give serious consideration to a suggestion by some of the pool members to create a new pool slot for an editor who would come to the Pentagon during a deployment to lend professional journalism help to the staff officers handling pool reports. Such a pool editor could edit copy, question content where indicated, and help expedite distribution of the reports.

13. The pool escorting system needs overhauling as well. There is no logical reason for the Washington-based escorts to be drawn from the top of

the Office of the ASD-PA Plans Division. The head of that division should remain in Washington to oversee getting out the pool products.

Pool escorts should be drawn from the most appropriate service, rather than limiting escort duty to officers of the Plans Division. The individual armed service public affairs offices should be required to assign military officers to the pool on a contingency basis. For example, if it's an Army operation, the escorts should be primarily Army officers. In the Panama deployment the three Washington-based escorts wore Air Force and Navy uniforms in what was an overwhelmingly Army operation.

Escorts should deploy in field uniforms or draw them from field commands soon after arriving. The Panama pool escorts wore uniforms befitting a day behind the desk at the Pentagon; this, I found, had a jarring effect on the Army people with whom they dealt.

14. The ASD-PA should close a major gap in the current system by requiring all pool participant organizations—whether print, still photo, TV, or radio—to share all pool products with all elements of the news industry. Pool participants must understand they represent the entire industry.

Any pool participant refusing to share with all legitimate requesters should be dropped from the pool and replaced by another organization that agrees to abide by time-honored pool practices.

15. There is merit in a suggestion by one of the pool photographers that participating news organizations share the cost of equipment such as a portable darkroom and a negative transmitter, which could be stored at Andrews AFB for ready access in a deployment. Other equipment essential for smooth transmission of pool products, such as satellite uplink gear, might also be acquired and stored in the same manner.

16. All pool-assigned reporters and photographers, not just bureau chiefs, should attend quarterly Pentagon sessions where problems can be discussed and rules and responsibilities underscored.

17. Public Affairs Officers from Unified Commands should meet periodically with pool-assigned reporters and photographers with whom they might have to work in some future crises.

■　■　■　■　■　■

Secretary of Defense Richard B. Cheney's Response:

I have read Mr. Hoffman's report. It's a good report. I don't agree with all facets of it in terms of recommendations. He interviewed me personally, and I told him that I specifically was the one who made the decision about whether or not to notify the pool and under what conditions and with how much lead time. That was my responsibility, and I accept whatever criticism goes with it.

If you go back and look at the sequence of events, the decision was made by the President basically on Sunday afternoon to conduct Operation Just Cause, to send forces into Panama. We did not actually undertake the operation until 1:00 Wednesday morning. So we had a couple of days as we built up the force and got ready actually to conduct the operation.

I was very concerned about the possibility of premature disclosure of the operation, that at some point Monday night or Tuesday morning I would turn on the television set and there would be in living color one of our correspondents standing up saying the United States military is getting ready to send forces into Panama. That would have created enormous problems for us, obviously, and also put at risk the lives of the men conducting the operation.

In addition to that, we had another problem, which was the weather problem. I was told on Monday, as a result of the weather forecast that predicted icing storms in North Carolina, that we might not be able to get the aircraft carrying the 82nd Airborne Division out of North Carolina in time to launch the operation Wednesday morning and that we might in fact have to delay 24 hours, which added some additional uncertainty in terms of making the decision as to when to notify the press.

In the final analysis, I made the judgment, based upon my concerns for premature disclosure, that we would not notify the press pool until after the close of the last evening news television broadcast, Tuesday evening. If I had acted sooner, then the press pool could have gotten to Panama earlier. As it was, they didn't get there until three or four hours after the operation commenced. I cannot say that we ran it perfectly. I'm sure there are places where we can improve upon the way we handled the press pool.

But in the final analysis, the choice for me comes down to the proposition of how much emphasis I want to place on accommodating the legitimate needs of the press to cover a significant military operation and my obligation to provide and guarantee as long as I can the security of an operation to protect the lives of the men that I send into combat. And given a choice or trade-off between those two obligations, you can be absolutely certain I will always come down on the side of protecting security as long as I can in order to safeguard those lives. That's my responsibility.

I have no problem trying to improve on the operation. We already have efforts under way by Assistant Secretary of Defense for Public Affairs Pete Williams to adopt some of the Hoffman recommendations that make sense. He's working with the joint staff in that regard.

But I will say that as long as I'm in this job, it's a decision I'm going to make on a case-by-case basis. Each circumstance is different and unique. We had the situation, for example, in connection with this particular callout that it was the week before Christmas. One of the calls went to a news bureau chief here in Washington and caught him in the middle of the office Christmas party. The assignment to go to Panama was shopped around the party. Now, fortunately, there was no immediate disclosure of that call. But it was not treated with the seriousness with which it has to be treated if the Secretary of Defense is going to have absolute confidence that his notifying the press won't lead to putting at risk the lives of the young men he sends into combat.

Again, I come back to the proposition that I'm eager to work with the press to find a way to make the pool as efficient as possible. I'm sure we can improve upon what happened in Panama, but in the final analysis my priorities are clear and nobody should be under any illusions about that.

The report by Mr. Hoffman was prepared in March 1990 at the behest of Mr. Pete Williams, the Assistant Secretary of Defense for Public Affairs. Its original title was "Review of Panama Pool Deployment, December 1989." The report appears here in slightly edited form. Mr. Cheney's response was made during the question-and-answer session following remarks before the American Society of Newspaper Editors in Washington, D.C., on 4 April 1990.

........9

The Media and Future Interventions: Scenario ....

By William A. Rusher

"The power of the media not merely to influence but to determine and even make events is growing. That is bound, in the end, to lead to a popular demand that it be subjected to more democratic control."

—Paul Johnson,
The Spectator, *1 November 1986*

At 10:00 A.M. EST on Wednesday, 15 February 1995, the President of the United States addressed the nation. His talk was carried on all major television and radio networks. It was brief and dramatic:

"My fellow Americans: As you know, our relations with Montegura have deteriorated gravely in recent years. The leftist regime, having consolidated its hold on the country after Congress ended military aid to the pro-democratic forces, has stepped up its pressure against its non-communist neighbors. Guerrilla forces based in Montegura, and supplied by leftist nations through that country, are gravely threatening the freely elected government of neighboring Monteverde through repeated bombings in its capital, and are also active in adjacent countries. I regret to say that there is evidence that revolutionary forces inspired by the anti-capitalist bloc are prepared to strike in our closest neighbor, Mexico, in the near future.

"The United States has repeatedly warned Montegura and its allies that we cannot tolerate the steady, indefinite expansion of their ideology by force

111

northward through Central America to our very border. In particular we have made it clear that the introduction of new weapon systems in that area would not be permitted, since they would fundamentally alter the strategic balance there.

"Despite these warnings, Montegura and its supporters have persisted in their attempts to destabilize the free and democratic countries to the north. And I very much regret to say that last week, in express disregard of our solemn and repeated warnings, three squadrons of deadly Cuban MiG-29s arrived at Monteguran military air bases in what is very clearly an attempt to change fundamentally the military balance in Central America.

"Under these circumstances, the United States is left no choice but to act before the situation becomes even worse and perhaps gets out of control altogether. Accordingly, after consultations with the National Security Council, the Joint Chiefs of Staff, the relevant Cabinet members, and leaders of both parties in both Houses of Congress, I have directed the armed forces of the United States to occupy the territory of the Republic of Montegura and secure it for the forces of freedom, in preparation for early elections to choose a new government. Operations to that end began just a little over four hours ago, and will continue until the assigned objectives have been achieved.

"I am confident that these steps will meet with the full approval of the American people, and that they will also be endorsed by Congress if they are still proceeding in 60 days when congressional approval of the overseas deployment of U.S. forces is required by the War Powers Act. Meanwhile, our hearts today are with our soldiers, sailors, airmen, and Marines, on whom so much depends. Let us pray that casualties on both sides will be light, that the battle will be over shortly, and that all of Central America will soon know, once again, the blessings of freedom.

"Thank you, and God bless America."

The first attacks of American forces—by landing craft on the coast of Montegura and by parachute and helicopter onto airfields which could then be used to fly in supplies—were almost uniformly successful, and the mood in the White House and the Pentagon was described as one of "cautious optimism." In Congress, only a handful of extreme leftist congressmen condemned the operation, while many in both parties praised it. A majority of members of the House and Senate, on both sides of the aisle, acknowledged privately that there seemed little else the President could do, in view of the brazen deployment of the MiG-29s.

The major media too, during that first week, contented themselves with reporting the military operations, with due regard for the security of troop movements, etc. In fact, just about the only discordant notes came from foreign sources. In a special emergency session, the UN Security Council, by a large margin, condemned the American attack. The nations voting for the resolution included some of America's closest allies, but the resolution was technically void because the U.S. representative vetoed it.

Reaction throughout much of the Third World was vociferously anti-American from the start. There were riots and anti-American demonstrations in several capitals: bombs exploded near the American embassies in six countries; and three U.S. Information Agency libraries were set ablaze. In NATO Europe, the gloom was intense; the conviction was widespread that the United States had committed a disastrous blunder. The British prime minister insisted on suspending judgment until the situation became clearer, but was hooted down in the House of Commons.

These negative reactions were, of course, duly reported to the American people by the media, but they had little effect as long as the news from the battlefront remained consistently upbeat.

During the second and third weeks of the invasion, the various fronts were stabilized. U.S. forces had consolidated their hold on much of the coast of Montegura and also over a portion of its northern sector. However, it had become apparent that the Monteguran armed forces, including their "international" component, weren't going to be any pushovers. The Montegurans were digging in grimly, and their large and well-equipped army was giving a good account of itself in pitched battles with U.S. forces. The U.S. Navy had, of course, effectively blockaded the country the moment hostilities began, and the Air Force could claim air supremacy over the battlefront most of the time, though antiaircraft missiles had managed, by the Pentagon's own admission, to shoot down six U.S. helicopters and three troop carriers.

Now, however, opposition to the invasion was increasing and mobilizing on the domestic Left. By mid-March demonstrations—small at first, but growing in size and number—were being staged in almost every major American city, and there were "teach-ins" or other protest actions on virtually every college campus. Television coverage of these was, of course, intensive. Abroad, too, the protests (and the riots and bombings) grew; one American military attaché was gunned down as he stepped out of his car.

In Congress, now, there was grumbling in the cloakrooms and the corridors. How long, exactly, did the President expect members of Congress to take this heat? Was this operation going to be a quick, surgical strike, on the order of a bigger Panama, or was it going to drag on for years, like Vietnam? Just how important was Montegura to American security anyway? It had been leftist-controlled for years, yet the world hadn't vanished in a blast of flame, had it? Certain prominent liberals in both the House and the Senate told their countrymen on the evening news programs of the major TV networks that the President owed the American people an explanation.

What, exactly, was the *goal* of this invasion? The people of Montegura certainly weren't welcoming our soldiers with open arms. Besides, three squadrons of fighter planes were scarcely much of a threat to American sovereignty in the skies. "How many more American soldiers," one Senator demanded, "will have to be shipped home in body bags before we learn why this invasion was necessary, or call a halt to it?"

Meanwhile, in neighboring Monteverde, guerrilla forces launched a massive campaign of terrorism, and the country's chief executive was assassinated. His successor declared a national state of emergency.

On 20 March, on the recommendation of the Joint Chiefs of Staff, the President authorized the commitment of 30,000 additional combat troops to augment the initial invasion force of 50,000, and called up elements of the Reserve and the National Guard. This, however, simply increased the protests in Congress, in the country at large, and abroad. "Where will it all end?" demanded one of television's most prominent anchormen, who thereupon decided to use that question as his sign-off words every night.

And now, as March drew toward a close and the enemy, though slowly giving ground, fought with desperate intensity, the mood of the American people turned somber. Casualty reports were now a familiar phenomenon, and every sizable American city counted its dead and wounded. On television, the grim reality of war was brought home to the public every night by newsmen the vast majority of whom had opposed the invasion, at least privately, from the very start.

From a crater carved by an exploding shell of a U.S. Navy battleship fired during the early days of the invasion, one TV correspondent picked up a fragment of shrapnel and held it out toward the camera. "This particular shell did no damage," he explained with a smile. "It landed here, in an empty field. The only losers were the taxpayers who paid for it in the first place. But another shell"—and here he gestured with the shrapnel—"scored a direct hit over there. On an orphanage."

One of the battleship's 16-inch guns had indeed, it seemed, by accident hit an orphanage in a nearby town where enemy soldiers were holding up the American advance. The scene now shifted to a makeshift hospital, where nursing nuns were caring for children injured by the shell. They had nothing to say to the American TV crew, but their looks—and the sad-eyed faces of the children—told volumes.

On another network that evening, the reporter was interviewing wounded American soldiers. Most of them were pretty matter-of-fact about it all. One young man with his arm in a sling just wanted to say hello to his folks back home. Another, who had lost a leg, was less exuberant. The war, he said, was "pretty bad." The camera moved on.

There was straight battle reportage too, of course: camera footage of American soldiers scurrying forward across a road and through a line of trees. ("The gooks are over there," a big black sergeant explained.) There was the sound of shots, and pictures of some sort of smoky fire. Then the reporter appeared onscreen: the village had been taken. Two American soldiers were dead. On, tomorrow, to the next village. But, "Where will it all end?"

By the beginning of April, five weeks into the invasion, polls indicated that most of the American people still supported it, but the percentage opposed had grown from 17 percent in late February to 26 percent in mid-March. Now it stood at 39 percent. In Congress, the rumbles had become a roar. Most congressmen, like most of the public, still supported the invasion, but they were growing increasingly uneasy as 25 April drew nearer—the 60th day of the operation and the one on which the President must, by law, recall America's troops unless Congress had by then authorized their continued deployment abroad.

Public uneasiness was heightened by a sharp resurgence of threatening military activity in the neighborhood of the Persian Gulf. Suddenly it seemed possible that what had begun as a quick, relatively painless military operation on our southern flank might become linked into a wider conflict, with incalculable consequences.

The savage week-long battle for possession of Montegura's capital, which ended in victory for the Americans on 7 April, was nevertheless depicted on American television as a disastrous defeat, because American casualties had been high. Closely paraphrasing Pyrrhus, one TV newsman declared that "one more such 'victory' and we will be ruined." His camera crew took Americans, watching horrified in their living rooms, on a grim tour of a road on the city's outskirts. Clearly visible were the bodies of seven American soldiers killed by a land mine. "I talked to this boy yesterday," the reporter mused, gesturing. "He was going to be married in September."

Another of the bodies was identified as that of Corporal Harry Flint, 22, of Rochester, New York. The scene switched to Rochester, where, by one of those miracles of modern television, Harry Flint's mother could now be seen, "live," watching this very program. A camera closed in tight on her homely face—puffy and red from weeping. But she was composed now, as she began to speak in a high-pitched, querulous voice.

"Harry loved the Army," she began. "He really loved it. I know, if he had to die, this . . . he would have"—her chin was trembling now—"I only hope, somehow, that some good comes of all this killing. I didn't want"—and now the eyes brim and overflow—"to lose my boy." She covers her sobbing face with her hands. (In December 1995 a special citation for distinguished reportage was awarded to the director of that program by a committee of the television industry.)

By coincidence it was later that very evening that another network carried an interview with the Monteguran foreign minister, taped through the facilities of the Canadian Broadcasting Corporation in Toronto. He was a mild-mannered, bespectacled man who spoke excellent English. He described mournfully the carnage the American invasion was causing in his country, and demanded reproachfully, "What have we done to you, to deserve this?" The interviewer raised the matter of the MiG-29s, only to be told that America's invasion proved why they were necessary—a point the interviewer seemed unable to refute. "Leave us in peace," the Monteguran begged; "we wish you no harm."

In vain the administration strove to remind the public of the stakes in this battle: was Central America going to become a forward base of an anti-capitalist, anti-democratic empire, armed with the most advanced weapons (and requiring, therefore, correspondingly advanced defenses), or wasn't it? The daily inundation of news from the battlefronts rubbed the public's nose in the human tragedy that war has always been—but which it had never before, even in Vietnam, so vividly and constantly been seen to be. As one furious general pointed out, a viewer watching the war on TV in his own home— morning, noon, and night—actually heard far more gunfire than the average combat infantryman, and saw more American corpses.

Television was, of course, the major medium that shaped American opinion, but the print media were not to be disregarded. And even radio, which receives far less attention than television but retains a vast audience and is dominated by producers, directors, and writers with exactly the same spectrum of leftist and liberal political attitudes, did its Herculean share. (One New York radio station began every news report from the battlefront with the deadpan phrase, "On the Monteguran killing ground. . . .")

By mid-April, America was a nation torn asunder. A little over half of the public sincerely believed that unless the invasion was carried through to a successful conclusion, the surprisingly resilient remnants of the Marxist-Leninist empire would have succeeded in planting a forward military base in America's own backyard, ready to create still further trouble in Mexico and elsewhere. About 40 percent (the rest "didn't know") believed, equally sincerely, that no military or diplomatic objective could possibly be worth the slaughter unfolding before their eyes on the evening news programs. In Congress, which was controlled by the opposition party, it now appeared that narrow majorities in both houses were prepared to deny authorization (required, after 60 days, by the War Powers Act) for the invasion to continue past 25 April. The President was staring disaster—military for the nation, political for himself—in the face.

On the morning of 18 April he summoned the owners of the major television networks, newsmagazines, wire services, and national newspapers to the White House for an all-day, off-the-record discussion. (Verbatim accounts of its key parts were published and broadcast the next day.)

"Ladies and gentlemen," the President began somberly, "I have asked you to come here to consult with me because this nation faces a crisis that is truly constitutional.

"None of us wishes our country ill. If we disagree, it is over means, not ends. I ask you, therefore, to believe me when I say that my military and civilian advisers and I—this administration, if you will—sincerely believed, and continue to believe, that the introduction of Cuban MiG-29s into Central America represented a threat so grave that it warranted an immediate military response. I may add that this belief was, at least until the middle of March, common ground between the two major parties, including the great majority of congressmen in both. That is why there was, in the beginning, as little opposition to the invasion, in Congress, as there was.

"But in the nearly two months since the invasion began, there has been a dramatic swing in public opinion. Although the military operations are succeeding and my military advisers tell me that we will prevail, casualties have been somewhat higher than expected and we are about four weeks behind our timetable. Far more ominously, public support for the invasion has fallen from over 80 percent at the outset to only a little over 50 percent today, and polls indicate that many of its critics are not only against it but furiously so.

"The reason is perfectly plain. Modern technology, which is nobody's fault, has made it possible for the news media to cover a war more rapidly, more intensively, and more vividly than ever before in history. The coverage of the Vietnam War, to which many people, rightly or wrongly, assign responsibility for America's failure to finish that job, was not half as effective, in terms of its impact on the home front, as the coverage of this invasion has already been.

"Now, the freedom of the American press is a precious thing. Certainly neither I nor any responsible member of my administration wants to infringe on it. Ordinarily, in any case, you can generally figure that in politics"—and here the President permitted himself a weary smile—"pressure from one side will tend to be canceled out by pressure from the other.

"But in the case of the major American media and this invasion, the fracture line runs, not through the media (which are now in almost unanimous opposition to the invasion), but between the media and certain of their allies on the one hand and, on the other, those groups and forces in American life that have normally supported me.

"Well, there's nothing wrong with that." (Another smile.) "I've been in this game too long to be surprised by, or angry at, opposition. But, ladies and gentlemen, we are approaching a point at which our media, dominated by people who are still in the minority politically, may nonetheless be able to impose their political will, thanks to the virtuosity of the news technologies they control. And I'm not sure that would be democracy.

"I have called you together, therefore—the people who, in effect, control what the American people see and hear about this war—to ask you to modify your reportage. I am not asking you to say or do anything that is false, or to suppress anything that is relevant. I *am* asking you to make your coverage better balanced, and to avoid taking cheap shots with what George Will once called 'the pornography of grief.' My military advisers estimate that we should be able to complete this operation by mid-July, but we can't do it by April 25th. Unless Congress authorizes continuation of the operation it will fail, Montegura will remain in the hands of virulently anti-democratic forces, all of our dead will have died for nothing, and the enemy's efforts to seize control of the rest of Central America and Mexico will have received an enormous boost. I can't believe," he concluded, "that you want that any more than I do."

There was a thick silence. Then a prominent publisher spoke up. "What bother some of us, Mr. President, are your assumptions. For example, plenty of people think your military advisers are wrong. What if there's no light at the end of the tunnel? What if this war drags on endlessly, like Vietnam, grinding up more and more human lives? And anyway, what makes you think that hostile regimes in Montegura and Monteverde necessarily mean hostile regimes in Mexico or other nearby countries? And if so, so what? The peoples of those countries have every right to decide for themselves what kind of government they want. If they decide they want to buy some MiGs to defend themselves (and I saw the Monteguran foreign minister on TV the other night who *pledged* they would only be used defensively), I say let 'em. The American people are turning against this war, and they're right."

There were murmurs of agreement around the long table. The President stared at the tabletop, then slowly replied. "You may be right. But the toughest thing about this job of mine is making the hard decisions. You know, Jimmy Carter said that all the easy decisions get weeded out on the way to the President's desk. The only ones that wind up here are the ones nobody else can make—or, perhaps, wants to make. And in this case I have made my decision. Now, under the law, Congress must ratify the decision within 60 days, by authorizing the further deployment of our forces abroad, or, in effect, reverse it. I don't think that law was such a hot idea, but it *is* the law, and I respect it as such. And Congress may very well refuse authorization to continue the operation beyond April 25th. Frankly, I think it *will* refuse, unless you people in the media lay off. No citizenry has ever had to undergo the kind of psychological assault and battery you have been subjecting the American people to in the last month or so. I seriously question whether any people ever ought to be compelled to."

"What about freedom of the press?" The speaker was the controlling stockholder of a major television network. "Are you telling us to shut up and put our tails between our legs and start praising this cockeyed expedition? Do you have any right to do such a thing? Anyway, even if we did what you want us to, I doubt our news staffs would go along. I think mine would walk right out from under me. And it'd be right."

"After all, Mr. President," another voice took up the argument, "these things that you don't like to see on TV or in the newspapers are happening. That's not our fault. We just report what's there to be reported."

"I don't think it's quite that simple, Pete," the President replied. "War is hell. We all know that. But one of your TV crews can go down there and make an important achievement like the capture of the Monteguran capital look like a disaster simply by concentrating on the American casualties."

"Suppose we do," someone else interjected, "—just for the sake of argument. Don't we have that right? Doesn't the First Amendment to the Constitution guarantee it? Even if we are in the minority as you contend, don't we have the right to be heard?"

Again the President spoke slowly. "You have the right to speak, of course. But what I am facing here is not simply opposition but something no President has ever faced before—certainly not to anything like this extent. I am facing a situation in which the entire American media, or at any rate virtually all of them that count in the shaping of public opinion, have not only chosen to oppose this operation but are very deliberately using their control over the dissemination of news about it to turn public opinion against it. In the present state of news technology, that amounts to the power to decide the issue. The power to broadcast and to publish has become, at least in certain circumstances, the power to destroy."

The discussion continued for several hours, more or less along the lines outlined above. Tempers grew heated; voices were raised. One or two of those invited to the White House tended to side with the President, and urged their colleagues to agree to modify their coverage of the invasion to reduce the amount of "tear-jerk stuff," as one publisher put it. But the great majority were unmoved. They actually broke into applause when one magazine owner told the President bluntly, "Face it: you don't have the country behind you on this one, and you should never have launched this invasion in the first place. Now your best bet is to end it as quickly as possible."

The President's face was hard, but his voice was almost inaudible as he responded. "Maybe so, Sam; maybe so. But I'm the guy who was elected President, and I swore to protect and defend the Constitution of this country to the best of my ability, so help me God. And I would urge you to look carefully at that Constitution. To be sure, the First Amendment says that 'Congress shall make no law abridging freedom of speech or of the press.' But neither it nor anything else in the Constitution places any limitation on the president in his capacity as commander in chief of the armed forces. We have had military censorship, to one degree or another, in every war we've ever waged. If Abraham Lincoln could suspend the writ of habeas corpus throughout the United States by executive proclamation and get away with it, I see no reason why I cannot, as commander in chief, limit far less extensively the right of journalists to brainwash the American public, by highly selective reportage, into bugging out on a military operation *in medias res*. And I might add that my attorney general agrees with me."

There was a long silence. Then somebody breathed, "You wouldn't dare."

"Wouldn't I?" the President retorted. "Want to try me?"

■　■　■　■　■　■

In considering the scenario above, it is important not to be distracted by irrelevancies. The scenario concerns a military operation against the fictitious country of Montegura in Central America, and therefore risks entanglement with the reader's particular attitudes to other U.S. interventions—actual or contemplated—in that area. It would be almost as easy, however, to devise a scenario involving an American military operation in the Middle East or Angola or the Philippines which would likewise pit an American president and his administration against the nation's dominant media.

Similarly, there is nothing inherently implausible, or even particularly strained, about the various journalistic tactics described. Many of them—e.g., the media's generous coverage of the accidental bombing of an orphanage, and the radio station that began each evening's news with the words "On the

Monteguran killing-ground . . ."—are modeled carefully on actual episodes during the Vietnam War or in more recent United States military operations.

The discussion between the embattled President and the media owners is intended only to present the two sides of the argument, with somewhat greater emphasis on the President's side because it is, of course, less widely or often heard in the country today. But I certainly don't mean to suggest that the dilemma, in our wide-open and lustily democratic society, is an easy one to resolve, still less that all justice is on one side or the other.

I *do* suggest that the present distribution of forces in American politics, in which presidents are often able to amass impressive electoral majorities, only to find the major media allied with their opponents and almost unanimously opposed to administration programs and goals, presents a very serious problem when the currently available techniques of news-gathering and news presentation are used by the media to turn public opinion against an ongoing military operation.

It is certainly not enough merely to quote the First Amendment, as the President in our scenario pointed out. There is another rule of law as old as Rome: *Salus populi suprema lex*—The safety of the people is the supreme law. What shall we do, if and when those two great principles collide?

It would be far better to face the matter now, and thrash it out as far as possible before the event, or we may find ourselves confronting it someday under far more urgent and much less satisfactory circumstances.

This article, originally chapter 11 of Mr. Rusher's book *The Coming Battle for the Media: Curbing the Power of the Media Elite* (Morrow, 1988), was reprinted in the September 1988 issue of *Parameters* under the title "The Media and Our Next Intervention: Scenario." The text has been revised and updated for the present book.

.... 10

The Military and the Media: A Troubled Embrace ....

By Bernard E. Trainor

At first they are polite, respectfully prefacing each question with "sir," but when faced with their own prejudices, the veneer of civility evaporates, hostility surfaces, and the questions give way to a feeding frenzy of accusations. No, these aren't journalists asking the questions. They are young officers and cadets, and I have experienced this phenomenon repeatedly when discussing relations between the military and the media at service academies and professional military schools. It is clear that today's officer corps carries as part of its cultural baggage a loathing for the press.

Indeed, military relations with the press—a term I apply to both print and television media—are probably worse now than at any period in the history of the Republic. I say this recognizing that Vietnam is usually cited as the nadir in military-media relations. But at least during the Vietnam War military men actually experienced what they judged to be unfair treatment at the hands of the Fourth Estate, and the issue was out in the open.

The majority of today's career officers, however, have had no such association with the press. Most of them were children during the war. In the case of those at the academies, some were probably still in diapers when Saigon fell. But all of them suffer this institutional form of post-traumatic shock syndrome. It is a legacy of the war, and it takes root soon after they enter service. Like racism, anti-Semitism, and all forms of bigotry, it is irrational but nonetheless real. The credo of the military seems to have become "duty, honor, country, and hate the media."

Although most officers no longer say the media stabbed them in the back in Vietnam, the military still smarts over the nation's humiliation in Indochina and still blames TV and the print media for loss of public support for the war. Today the hostility manifests itself in complaints that the press will not keep a secret and that it endangers lives by revealing details of sensitive operations. The myth of the media as an unpatriotic, left-wing, anti-military establishment is thus perpetuated.

Having spent most of my adult life in the military and very little of it as a journalist, I am more qualified to comment on military culture than that of the media. I must admit that in the post-Vietnam years I too was biased against the press. But having had feet in both camps gives me a unique perspective which I now try to share with each, particularly the military.

Did the press stab the military in the back during Vietnam? Hardly. The press initially supported the war, but as casualties mounted and the Johnson Administration failed to develop a coherent strategy to bring the war to a satisfactory conclusion, the press became critical. Whether the press influenced public opinion or simply reflected it will be argued for years to come. But it was a misguided policy that was primarily at fault for the debacle, not the media.

The media was, however, guilty of instances of unfair and sensational reporting which veterans of that war still resent. This was particularly true in the latter stages, when the nation was weary of nightly war news and when cub newspaper and television journalists tried to make headlines out of thin gruel. More responsible supervision should have been exercised by editors, but it was not, and many in the military, already frustrated by the war, felt the press as a whole was deliberately trying to humiliate them.

The legacy of the war sharpened the tension which exists between the media and the military, but it is not its cause. The roots of tension are in the nature of the institutions. The military is hierarchical with great inner pride and loyalties. It is the antithesis of a democracy—and must be so if it is to be effective. It is action-oriented and impatient with outside interference. Many things it legitimately does make little sense to civilians who have scant knowledge of military matters. The military wants only to be left alone to carry out its assigned mission.

To the contrary, a free press—one of the great virtues and elemental constituents of a democracy—is an institution wherein concentration of power is viewed as a danger. The press is a watchdog over institutions of power, be they military, political, economic, or social. Its job is to inform the people about the doings of their institutions. By its very nature, the press is skeptical and intrusive. As a result there will always be a divergence of interests between the media and the military. That they are both essential to the well-being of our nation is beyond question, but the problem of minimizing the natural friction between the two is a daunting one.

The volunteer force in a subtle way has contributed to this friction. At the height of the cold war and throughout the Vietnam War, the military was at the forefront of American consciousness. Scarcely a family did not have a son or loved one liable to the draft. The shadow of national service cast itself over the family dinner table and generated in virtually all Americans a real and personal interest in the armed forces. This interest was heightened by the experiences and memories of fathers and older brothers who had fought in World War II and Korea and who maintained a lively interest in soldiering. With the end of the draft and the advent of a volunteer army this awareness disappeared, along with the pertinence of the older generation of warriors. Only the families of those who volunteered for the service kept touch with the modern Army.

The military, which for so long had been bound to civil society, drifted away from it. Military bases were few and far between and located in remote areas unseen by much of urban and suburban America. A large percentage of volunteer servicemen married early and settled down to a life where their base and service friends were the focal points of their lives. No longer did uniformed soldiers rush home on three-day passes whenever they could get them. When servicemen did go home, they did so wearing civilian clothes and, given the somewhat more tolerant attitude of the military toward eccentricity in dress and hair style, they were no longer as sharply marked by short haircuts and shiny shoes. Off post they were nearly indistinguishable in appearance from their civilian cohort.

To the average civilian, the term *military* soon came to be equated with the Pentagon, with fearsome intercontinental missiles, and with $600 toilet seats and other manifestations of waste, fraud, and abuse. The flesh-and-blood association the civilian formerly had with the armed forces atrophied, and he came to regard the military as just another bureaucracy. For its part, the military settled into the relative isolation of self-contained ghettos and lost touch with a changing America. It focused on warlike things and implicitly rejected the amorality of the outside world it was sworn to defend. In an age of selfishness, the professional soldier took pride in his image of his own selflessness. A sense of moral elitism emerged within the armed forces which is apparent today to any civilian who deals with those institutions. The all-volunteer force not only created a highly competent military force, it also created a version of Cromwell's Ironside Army, contemptuous of those with less noble visions. It is no wonder that those who chose the profession of arms looked with suspicion upon those members of the press who pried into their sacred rituals.

Oddly enough I have found striking similarities between my colleagues in both camps. Both are idealistic, bright, totally dedicated to their professions, and technically proficient. They work long hours willingly under arduous conditions, crave recognition, and feel they are underpaid. The strain on family life is equally severe in both professions. But there are notable differences as well. A journalist tends to be creative, while a soldier is more content with traditional approaches. Reporters are independent, while military men are team players. And of course one tends to be liberal and skeptical, the other conservative and accepting.

There is another big difference which bears directly on their interrelationship. The military is hostile toward the journalist, while the journalist is indifferent toward the military. To the journalist, the military is just another huge bureaucracy to report on, no different from Exxon or Congress. But whereas businessmen and politicians try to enlist journalists for their own purposes, the military man tries to avoid them, and when he cannot, he faces the prospect defensively with a mixture of fear, dread, and contempt.

Most of my military brothers in arms would be surprised to know that when asked for an opinion about the military profession, young journalists having no prior association with the military rate career officers highly. They view officers as bright, well-educated, dedicated, and competent, although they wonder why anyone would make the service a career. Their prejudgment of enlisted personnel is far less flattering. Most journalists—mistakenly, of course—have the image of an enlisted man as a disadvantaged, not-too-bright high-school dropout who comes from a broken home and cannot fit into society.

Ask a journalist for his opinion of servicemen after his first reporting assignment on the military, and the view will be radically different. The journalist will lavishly praise the enlisted personnel he met and relate how enthusiastic they were. He will remark how well they knew their jobs. He'll note how proud they were of what they were doing, and how eager they were to explain their duties. Genuine admiration and enthusiasm come through in the reporter's retelling of his encounters. But what of the officers? "The officers? . . . Oh, they're a bunch of horses' asses."

To understand such a critical assessment of officers, one only has to take a hypothetical, though typical, walk in a journalist's shoes as he goes for his first interview with a senior officer. In this interview, it happens to be a general:

After a seemingly endless round of telephone calls to set up the interview, you arrive—a well-disposed journalist, notebook and tape recorder in hand—at headquarters. You are met by a smiling public affairs officer who signs you in and gets you a pass. You then are led through a series of offices under the baleful stare of staff factotums, while your escort vouches for the legitimacy of your alien presence. At last you arrive at a well-appointed anteroom where everyone speaks in hushed, reverent tones.

After a wait, the door to a better-appointed office opens, and you are ushered in with the announcement, "THE GENERAL will see you now." Not knowing whether to prostrate yourself or simply to genuflect, you enter the sanctum sanctorum vaguely aware of others entering with you, but grateful for their presence. Graciously received by the General, you are invited to sit down THERE, while the General resumes his place behind his imposing desk backed by colorful flags and martial memorabilia. In addition to the General and the public affairs officer, there are several other officers of varied ranks present to whom you are not introduced. All of them take seats at the nod of the General, one of whom places himself facing the General but slightly to your rear, at the outer edge of your peripheral vision.

Following introductory pleasantries, the interview gets underway. You set your tape recorder on the coffee table and open your notebook. This triggers a duplicate reaction on the part of those around you, and an elaborate choreography begins. Your tape recorder is immediately trumped by at least two others, and the General's entourage poises with pencils and yellow legal pads to take notes of the proceedings. Throughout the interview, marked by elliptical responses to your questions, you are aware of knowing looks, nods, and shrugs being exchanged around the room. More disconcerting is the series of hand and arm signals being given to the General by the officer sitting to the rear, in the manner of an operatic prompter. You are given your allotted time down to the second, at which time you are escorted out of the office as the General returns to important matters of state.

After turning in your badge and being bidden a good day, you are back out on the street wondering what it was all about. Why all the lackeys? Were they hiding something? Why the signals? Didn't the General know enough about the subject to discuss it without a prompter? Puzzled, you walk away wondering whether your host was a charlatan or a fool.

Obviously the little scenario above is an exaggeration, but those who have been through the process know that it is just barely so.

The attitude of the military is bound to affect that of the press and vice versa. If it is one of mutual suspicion and antagonism, the relationship will never improve, and in the end the American public will be the loser.

There is nothing more refreshing than an open relationship. Senior officers know their business and can talk about it sensibly without a bunch of flacks around. Journalists know that some topics are off-limits in any meeting with the press, and they respect the obligation of a military officer not to disclose information he should not. It is a poor journalist indeed who tries to trap an officer into a disclosure that is legitimately classified. The counterbattery of tape recorders and legions of witnesses are of course intended as protective devices in case a journalist does a hatchet job on the person he is interviewing. This is useless protection, however, because if a reporter is out to paint a deliberately unfair picture of a person or institution, he will do it regardless of recorded safeguards of accuracy. The best protection against the unscrupulous few is not to deal with them.

Each of the services has expended great effort at improving military-media relations. Public affairs officers are trained at Fort Benjamin Harrison, and all major commands have graduates of the school to act as a bridge between the warrior and the scribe. Installations and war colleges sponsor symposia and workshops to improve relations with the media. Special tours of military installations and activities are conducted for the press by the Defense Department and the services, and some components of the Fourth Estate even reciprocate. But these efforts have little effect on military attitudes and make few military converts because most of them end up focusing on the mechanics of the interrelationship rather than its nature. Discussing how best to improve military press pool coverage in the wake of Panama, while a useful exercise, does little to minimize the underlying prejudice between the two institutions, much less eliminate it.

What is frequently overlooked by the military is that the profession of journalism is as upright as that of the military, with pride in its integrity and strict norms of conduct for its members. For example, it is absolutely forbidden at *The New York Times* to secretly tape an interview, by phone or in person, or to mislead a source as to the identity of the reporter. Most newspapers have similar restrictions. As a result there are few instances of yellow journalism today. The journalistic world knows who the unscrupulous are within its ranks and gives them short shrift. An unscrupulous journalist will never last on a reputable paper, and advertisers upon whom a newspaper depends for its existence are not inclined to place ads in papers with a reputation for unfair reporting.

This is not to say that journalists will shy from using every legitimate means to dig out a story. The reputation of government agencies, including the military, for overclassifying, for withholding the truth, and for putting a spin on events is well known, and a good reporter will never take things at face value. The tendency of journalists to disbelieve half of what they are told also adds to the military's paranoia.

There is no question, of course, that some journalists go too far in reporting a story, and so do some newspapers. Journalism, besides being a professon, is also a business, and businesses must show profit. This leads to fierce competition. A scoop means sales, sales mean profits, and that is what free enterprise is all about. For a reporter it also means reputation, and if his editors were not pushing him for exclusive stories he would be pushing himself so as to enhance his reputation and maybe win a Pulitzer prize. Thus a journalist may uncover a story relating to national security which would jeopardize that security if it were made public. This is particularly true if it is on operational matters, the favorite complaint of today's officer corps. In his eagerness to be on the front page, the journalist may disregard the security sensitivity of his story and file it to his newspaper. But that is where editors come in. They are mature people with long years in the business and good judgment on the implications of a story. In truly critical instances an editor will withhold a damaging story.

The record of the American press in this regard is good, despite unsubstantiated claims made by military officers that the press leaks operational information. Let two examples suffice to illustrate the point. Newsrooms knew beforehand of the planned airstrikes on Libya in 1986 and held the news until the raids had taken place so as not to endanger the air crews. Likewise, every

Washington newsman knew that Marine Lieutenant Colonel William R. Higgins had held a sensitive job in the office of the Secretary of Defense immediately prior to his United Nations assignment in Lebanon, where he was kidnapped and later executed. Yet in hopes that his captors would remain ignorant of this possibly compromising information, no mention was made of it in the American press until after it appeared in a Lebanese newspaper.

Whether the press acted responsibly during the December 1989 Panama invasion, when it reported air movement of troops on the night of the operation, is the latest subject of debate. News of the airlift was on television before H-Hour, but nothing was said of a planned airborne assault. Whether anyone in the press knew for certain that an assault was about to take place is in doubt, but if it was known, nothing was disclosed publicly. The air activity was alternately reported as a buildup for military action or part of the war of nerves against the Noriega regime. Our government itself actually contributed to the "leak" with its cute reply to newsmen's questions about the unusual air movements. The government spokesman said they were routine readiness exercises unrelated to Panama, but he withdrew the "unrelated to Panama" part of his statement *prior* to the assault the following day, thus giving away the show.

On the whole the military was satisfied with press coverage of its Panama intervention. Certainly Just Cause received more favorable reporting than the Grenada operation in 1983. However, the one vehicle designed to improve military-media relations during military operations was a failure—the press pool.

The idea of a press pool came about as the result of the exclusion of journalists from the Grenada operation. At the time, the press howled that the people had the right to know what their armed forces were doing and that journalists should not be denied entry to a war zone. The press concluded that they were shut out more to cover up military incompetence than to preserve operational security. They were more convinced of it when stories of that incompetence surfaced. As a result, DOD-sponsored press pools were established to allow selected journalists from the various media to represent the press as a whole during future operations. The pool reporters were rotated periodically and were told to be ready on short notice to accompany military units. A list of names was held at the Pentagon for that purpose. They were not to be told beforehand where they were going or what was about to happen.

The system was tested in some peacetime readiness exercises to everybody's satisfaction. But in its first real test, during the 1987–88 operations in the Persian Gulf, reporters complained that they were isolated from the action and kept ignorant of events. Many complained that their military hosts were more interested in brainwashing them than exposing them to the news.[1]

Panama was the second test, and again the pool concept failed.[2] Reporters were flown to Panama but kept at Howard Air Force Base and given briefings during the highpoints of the operation. When they were finally taken into

Panama City, it was to view events and locations of little news value. Meanwhile, journalists not in the pool were streaming into Panama on their own and providing vivid firsthand accounts of the action. Pool reporters cried foul. The military, for their part, complained that the pool journalists made unreasonable demands for transportation and communications facilities and that they were callous of the dangers involved in taking them to scenes of fighting. Nobody was or is happy with the pool arrangement.

The pool concept suffers three fatal flaws. The first is that the military is always going to want to put on its best face in hopes of influencing the reporters it is hosting. When the military is faced with the choice of taking a reporter to the scene of a confused and uncertain firefight or to the location of a success story—well, take a wild guess which the military will choose, regardless of its relative newsworthiness. Second, because the military brings pool reporters to the scene of action, it also feels responsible for transporting them around, and this may not be logistically convenient at times. Third, the military is protective and feels responsible for the safety of any civilians they are sponsoring. Keeping the press pool isolated at an air base in Panama was a genuine reflection of military concern for the reporters' safety. It is only during long campaigns like Vietnam that the protective cloak wears thin, and then usually because journalists find ways of getting out from under the military's wing.

Implicit in the military attitude toward the pool is not only its institutional sense of responsibility, but also its lack of understanding of journalists. If the pool is to work better, the services must recognize that they have no obligation to the pool other than to get them to the scene of the action and brief them on the situation. Beyond that, reporters are on their own. They are creative people who can take care of themselves. Any additional assistance rendered is appreciated but not necessary; it certainly doesn't provide grounds to restrict coverage of the story. Naval operations and in some instances air operations can be an exception because no facilities may be available other than those aboard ships or in a plane. But as the Persian Gulf illustrated, journalists proved to be a resourceful lot by hiring civilian helicopters to overfly the fleet—even at the risk of being shot down.

The press, on the other hand, should be selective in whom they send to war. Pool membership should require a physically fit, versatile journalist who knows something about the military. Few reporters have previous military experience, unfortunately, and few editors can afford the luxury of a military specialist on their payrolls. But the Defense Department would be happy to provide pool members with orientations and primers on military matters. At least then a reporter could learn some military jargon and the difference between a smoke grenade and a fragmentation grenade.

Old-timers long for the days of Ernie Pyle and Drew Middleton, when the military and the press saw events as one, and there was a love bond between the two. In those days the military could do no wrong—but even if it did, a censor saw to it that the public did not find out about it. Those were the days when the nation was on a holy crusade against the evil machinations of Fascism and Nazism. In this desperate struggle, propaganda was more important than truth. Had it been otherwise, many of the World War II heroes we revere today would have been pilloried by the press as butchers and bunglers.

Today's generals have no such friendly mediation. Moral crusades are no longer the order of the day, and unquestioned allegiance to government policy died with our involvement in Vietnam. The government lied once too often to the American people and lost their confidence. Today the press does what Thomas Jefferson envisaged for it when he rated it more important than the Army as a defender of democratic principles. It keeps a sharp eye on the military and on the government it serves.

This should not dismay the professional soldier.[3] After all, parents have a right to know what the military is doing to and with their sons and their tax money. If the services act responsibly and honestly, even with mistakes, there is little to fear from the press.

This is the challenge to today's and tomorrow's military leaders. They must work to regain the respect and confidence of the media as their predecessors once had it in the dark days of a long-ago war. The press is not going to go away. Hence, the anti-media attitude that has been fostered in young officers must be exorcised if both the military and the media are to serve well the republic for which they stand.

Notes

1. See Barry E. Willey, "Military-Media Relations Come of Age," *Parameters,* 19 (March 1989), 76–84 (reprinted in chapter 7 of this volume); Tom Ahern, "White Smoke in the Persian Gulf," *Washington Journalism Review,* 9 (October 1987), 18; and Mark Thompson, "With the Press Pool in the Persian Gulf," *Columbia Journalism Review* (November/December 1987), 46.

2. Fred S. Hoffman, "Review of Panama Pool Deployment, December 1989," Memorandum for Correspondents, the Pentagon, Washington, D.C., 20 March 1990 (reprinted in chapter 8 of this volume).

3. For a skeptical and remarkably candid view by a serving officer of today's military-media relations, see Major General Patrick H. Brady, "Telling the Army Story: 'As It Is, Not As It Should Be,' " *Army,* September 1990, pp. 22–45. General Brady was the Army's chief of public affairs during 1987–90.

This article appeared originally in the December 1990 issue of *Parameters.*

.... 11

Soldiers and Scribblers Revisited: Working with the Media ....

By Richard Halloran

© *1991 Richard Halloran*

After World War II, General Dwight D. Eisenhower wrote in his book, *Crusade in Europe:* "The commander in the field must never forget that it is his duty to cooperate with the heads of his government in the task of maintaining a civilian morale that will be equal to every purpose."[1] The principal agency to accomplish that task, the general said, was the press. He asserted that the commander should recognize the press's mission in the war and assist them in carrying it out. Throughout his military campaigns, General Eisenhower said, "I found that correspondents habitually responded to candor, frankness, and understanding."[2]

Relations between the military forces and the press have come a long way since those thoughtful and temperate words, and most of it has been downhill. In the Gannett Center for Media Studies at Columbia University, Liz Trotta, a veteran television reporter who conducted assessments of military-media relations, said in April 1990 she had concluded "that the relationship between the military and the media is at its most distant and cantankerous since the Civil War."[3] That was before the deployment of American forces to Saudi Arabia and the Persian Gulf, where coverage, in the early days at least, seemed balanced. In Washington, the press occasionally

131

sniped at President Bush's policy but generally the coverage reflected the public's support for him.

Even so, the ill will between the military and the press will probably continue unabated. One reason is that the Vietnam generation has come of age in journalism, as in the military service and other sectors of American life. Newspapers and television in the United States today are run largely by people who sat out the war in Vietnam or actively opposed the American engagement. This generation is either apathetic about American soldiers and sailors or openly antagonistic to anything connected with military power. Consequently, even as many correspondents seek to play it straight, some of today's military reporting and editing borders on intellectual dishonesty.

Nevertheless, soldiers cannot avoid dealing with the scribblers of the press or the talking heads of television. To think otherwise would be naive. After a dinner with senior officers at Fort Leavenworth several years ago, a colonel challenged a correspondent: "Why should I bother with you? My job is to train troops to go to war." It was a pertinent question. On the positive side, as General Eisenhower pointed out, the press is a vital channel of communication within Clausewitz's trinity of government, the army, and the people. The scribblers squirt grease into that machinery to help make it go. On the negative side, the scribblers can also throw sand into the machinery. If military officers refuse to respond to the press, they are in effect abandoning the field to critics of the armed forces. That would serve neither the nation nor the military services. In this situation, the initiative must come mostly from military officers because the scribblers own the presses, buy ink by the 55-gallon drum, and have shown little inclination in recent years to develop professional relations with soldiers.

As Elie Abel, the TV correspondent and later dean of Columbia's Graduate School of Journalism, once wrote about the press: "Its instinctive rejection of self-improvement schemes as far back as the Hutchins Commission in 1947 leaves little room for hope of wholesale reform."[4] Thus officers should accept the press as it is, whether that seems fair or not. They should learn to work with this flawed institution and seek over time to persuade journalists to be aware of military concerns. What follows, then, is one scribbler's suggested guidance to military officers on dealing with the press and television. Most of these suggestions apply in war, contingency operations, and peace.

• **Quit Bellyaching.** An anti-press bias akin to the mindless hostility of anti-Semitism or anti-Catholicism runs through much of the officer corps today. Part of the cause is, obviously, the search for a scapegoat for the defeat in Vietnam. Curiously, that antipathy is often more virulent among younger officers who never served in Vietnam than among more mature officers.

More disdain is generated by the traditional suspicion of soldiers for civilians, in this case for civilians who write critically or expose things that soldiers would prefer to be kept secret. Still more appears to arise from ignorance among officers of the First Amendment and the role of the press in

America. And not a small amount is a reaction to excesses in certain elements of the press and television.

Like other citizens, military officers are surely entitled to their opinions. But the constant outpouring of vitriol upon the press does little to protect the armed forces from the abuses of the press or to provide for a professional working relationship with journalists who play it straight. In sum, bellyaching about the press is much like cursing at a Sunday school picnic: It sounds like hell and doesn't do a damn bit of good.

- **Never Lie.** In a luncheon address to the National Press Club in October 1988, General Colin L. Powell, then the President's national security adviser, said: "I do not believe a public official, . . . having sworn an oath to the Constitution and the people of the United States, has any part in any set of circumstances to lie, either to Congress or to the press."[5] The general was right, idealistically and practically. Lying to the press is not important in itself. But an officer lying through the press to the people he has sworn to defend soils his uniform and violates the time-honored code dictating that officers do not lie, cheat, or steal.

Moreover, the liar will most likely get caught sooner or later, as witness Rear Admiral John Poindexter and Lieutenant Colonel Oliver North. No good reporter takes information from one source; rather, he checks with as many sources as possible to confirm and round out the story. Further, there is always tomorrow for a reporter to discover and correct today's lies or bad information. When that happens, the liar can expect to see his name in print. The fact of his lie will spread and he will lose his credibility, rendering him useless to his service and the armed forces as a source of information. Nor should an officer lie if asked about classified information; he can say: "I'm not at liberty to discuss that subject." The standard policy of neither confirming nor denying the presence of nuclear weapons could be used as an example in other cases.

Since deception is a basic principle of war, what about lying to deceive the enemy? That is not permissible when it goes through the press and deceives American citizens. The lie would not only be dishonorable but would erode the credibility of the military service once the lie has been discovered. But what if a lie is deemed necessary to save the lives of troops? I suggest taking the reporter aside to tell him the truth, warning him of the clear and present danger to life if he prints the story in question. Avoid the tired catchall "national security." It is vague and has been abused so often that no reporter worth his salt will pay attention. If that warning does not work, get a senior general or civilian official to call the top editor or producer. The history of the American press is replete with examples of sensitive information being voluntarily withheld for good reason, though this fact is not widely known. If a publication refuses to withhold the information—and there are a few that would refuse—the only recourse is for the military to change its operational plans. In such cases, the operation has probably already been compromised anyway.

What if an officer is ordered to lie? Treat that as any other illicit order, pointing out why it would be wrong, appealing to higher authority if necessary, and being prepared to take the consequences if the order stands. It is a sad commentary on the state of military ethics that this issue need be addressed at all. But it is necessary because many officers have suggested that lying to the press would be permissible.

• **MYOB.** The time-tested advice to mind your own business, often applied in other contexts, works here. Officers will rarely misstep if, in interviews with the press, they stick to what they know and to subjects appropriate to their rank and position.

The unfortunate case of General Michael J. Dugan, the former Chief of Staff of the Air Force, is instructive. General Dugan, interviewed by three reporters aboard a plane returning from Saudi Arabia, got fired because Secretary of Defense Richard Cheney thought the general had overstepped the mark. Mr. Cheney asserted that the general, who spoke on the record, had discussed strategic decisions that were not his to make, had disclosed classified information, and had commented on the operations of other services. Senior Air Force officers said later the journalists had abided by agreed ground rules and normal journalistic practices, and even checked with the general's staff to ascertain that he had been quoted accurately and in context.

General Dugan's remarks, which appeared in Sunday editions of *The Washington Post* and the *Los Angeles Times*, were promptly disavowed on a television news program by Brent Scowcroft, the President's national security adviser. The next day General Dugan was dismissed in a penalty that, in this writer's view, was unduly harsh. The nation, the military services, and the Air Force lost because General Dugan had come to office armed with a plan intended to tell the Air Force's story better. His approach was a breath of fresh air after the stifling policy of his predecessor, General Larry D. Welch.

Ironically, in the same Sunday edition of the *Los Angeles Times* containing the report on General Dugan was an interview with Army Chief of Staff General Carl E. Vuono, who was also confronted with some sensitive issues. But General Vuono, asked about a residual force staying in Saudi Arabia, said, "I'm not going to get into that." Queried on a political issue, the general said, "I'm not going to comment." But asked about the shape of the Army over the next five years, General Vuono gave an answer that many in Congress might not like: "If we're forced to take some of the deep cuts that some folks have talked about, and you're not going to have a trained and ready Army, the nation is going to be the loser."[6]

The lesson to be drawn from this comparison—a comparison intended not to be invidious in any way—is this: Do not avoid the press, but when talking with correspondents stick to what is proper for soldiers to talk about.

Some years ago, Secretary of Defense Harold Brown, not wanting to answer a question I had asked, leaned back in his chair and said: "Dick, the First Amendment gives you every right to ask that question. But there's nothing in the First Amendment that says I have to answer it."

• **Develop an IFF.** With devices known as "Identification, Friend or Foe," soldiers determine who is an ally and who an enemy. In the same way, an officer should always know to whom he or she is talking in the press. Is the reporter experienced in military matters or a novice? Do the reporter and his editors play it straight, or do they have their own agenda? It's easy to get a line on a reporter and publication or TV station because the track record is there for everyone to see. If the reporter is not known in Camp Swampy, a few phone calls into the network of public affairs officers should produce a clear picture.

Many officers, infected with the pervasive anti-press virus, fail to distinguish between journalists who play it straight and those who don't. Therefore they needlessly antagonize those who seek to render honest accounts. Officers should thus respond to experienced, reputable reporters in a courteous, straightforward manner. Approach a novice or sloppy journalist carefully. Refuse to truck with hostile muckrakers unless you absolutely must.

• **Differentiate.** During the deployment of battalions from the 82nd Airborne and 7th Divisions to Honduras in March 1988, the Army herded a gaggle of print and TV reporters, still photographers, and cameramen into a chopper and dropped them on a hapless company in the field. It was a mess. Reporters stumbled over one another, cameramen and photographers shoved each other, and the troops were bewildered by the turmoil. It would have been far better to have sorted the gaggle into groups with similar interests and spread them out among different units.

Too many officers, including public affairs officers who should know better, lump all journalists together whether they are from print or television, from general papers or trade magazines, from the newsroom or editorial board, or from the ranks of columnists or straight reporters. In reality, journalists are as different as paratroopers and tankers, soldiers and sailors. They have different needs and ways of working. In simple terms, newspaper reporters need to talk to people while a television team needs pictures. Too often officers are so caught up in getting camera positions for television people that they don't have time to answer real questions from the print reporters.

• **Set Firm Ground Rules.** Before you begin talking with a journalist, have a specific understanding on the rules of engagement. Since no two journalists or officials agree on the exact meaning of code words, be precise. "On the record" means you can be quoted by name, rank, and serial number. After that it gets fuzzy; perhaps the most misunderstood term is "off the record." For many officers, it means merely: "Don't quote or identify me." But "off the record" really means the correspondent may not report the information nor use it to pry out information elsewhere. Go off the record only with a reporter you trust; never go off the record with a group of reporters. Off the record should be confined to private conversations intended to clarify a point, to explain something that cannot be made public, or to keep the reporter from stumbling into a mistake. Most good reporters will not agree to go off the record except with sources they trust not to sandbag them.

"Background" usually means something like "a senior Army officer" or "a policymaking Pentagon official." "Deep background" was crafted to permit reporters to use information without leaving any trace of the source; this insidious form of sourcing allows officials to float viewpoints without taking responsibility for them. But it has become ingrained in Washington, largely because the press acquiesces.

If you violate ground rules to which you have agreed, expect to see your name in print. Sources cannot speak without attribution one day and then deny the story the next day. If a reporter violates the ground rules, chew his butt, report it to his superiors and competitors, but never speak to him again.

- **Speak English.** Every profession has its own jargon—law, medicine, military service, even journalism. Specialized language may ease communication within a profession, although that is debatable when acronyms intended to speed communication become so arcane as to require dictionaries.

Jargon, however, impedes communication with the outside world. Thus, speak in plain English and be prepared to explain the meaning of military language. Be especially alert to inexperienced reporters who may be diffident about showing their ignorance. But be prepared for more seasoned correspondents to interrupt you in mid-sentence to ask for an explanation.

Be particularly careful in briefings for journalists. Military briefings are intended to transmit large doses of information in a compact time. But that format sometimes overwhelms the listener, especially if he or she is not experienced in such briefings. It can go a long way toward ensuring accuracy if the briefer provides a hard copy of the slides. This allows the reporter to concentrate his note-taking on the briefer's remarks.

Robert Sims, a top Navy public affairs officer and later Assistant Secretary of Defense for Public Affairs, gave the best advice in a book about the Pentagon press corps: "Precision is the vital ingredient in the relationship."[7]

- **Anticipate.** At the public rollout of the M-1 Abrams tank, the vehicle was put through its paces, including a run up a steep ramp. When the tank stopped just below the lip of the ramp, some reporters thought it had stalled. That sent Army officers, who had failed to anticipate the question, scurrying about explaining that the test had come off as planned.

Journalists do not see the world as soldiers see it. Yet officers who spend their careers making estimates of the situation get caught off guard by the press every day. Officers for whom making contingency plans is second nature are rarely ready to combat leaks or unfavorable publicity. For all senior officers, I suggest a check: before you sign off on a decision, ask yourself what it will look like on the front page of tomorrow's newspaper. If it will look good, fine. If not, reconsider the decision. If it's necessary nonetheless, prepare to defend it if it becomes public. Do not wait until it becomes news to start dealing with adverse reactions.

In addition, be prepared for leaked or adversarial accounts to be incomplete and out of context. In some cases, the best defense may be a preemptive strike by announcing the decision. Even if it is not of immediate interest to the press, which is a hard judgment for soldiers to make, you will have erred on the side of prudence. If the decision later becomes controversial, you can point to the earlier effort to make it known.

Public affairs officers should advise their commanders to anticipate. But too many PAOs sit on their duffs waiting for things to happen instead of gathering intelligence on news about to break.

• **React Faster.** It is an imperfect world and even officers who anticipate will sometimes get blindsided by an adverse leak or a critical report. Responsible reporters will call the military for a defense or rebuttal; responsible officers will make sure the reporters get it before the sun goes down. If not by then, any rebuttal will be lost in the wind. One afternoon in Washington, critics of the Navy put out a report asserting that the new Aegis cruiser was top-heavy and might capsize in a storm. Calls to the Navy for comment or evidence to refute the charge went unanswered for more than 24 hours. By that time, the story had come and gone and the Navy never caught up with it.

If an irresponsible reporter prints a story without getting your side of it, a simple denial the next day will not do. Find a way to plow new ground and thus warrant another story with fresh information, including your side of yesterday's story. When something goes wrong—a training accident, for example—don't wait for the first phone call. Get the facts, work up the best explanation you can at the time, and go public. Announce that not all the information is in and tell reporters that the episode will surely look different as it develops.

The former Chairman of the Joint Chiefs of Staff, Admiral William J. Crowe, did a masterful job of briefing the press a few hours after the cruiser *Vincennes* mistakenly shot down an Iranian airliner. Throughout his briefing, the admiral warned that the findings were preliminary and that many questions remained unanswered. Unsophisticated accounts later tried to make much of what proved to be erroneous information, but the good reporters noted only that the account had changed as better information came in.

• **Leak.** At a seminar with the National Security Fellows at Harvard, an Air Force officer asked: "You say that officers should be ethical and not lie to the press. But you advocate leaking to the press. Isn't that contradictory? Isn't leaking a form of lying or cheating?" It was an incisive question and the answer is a tough call. A fine line runs between educating journalists and leaking to them. The first means giving correspondents the general background they need to improve their coverage. Leaks, however, are connected with specific issues and are intended to influence the course of events.

Judicious leaking is permissible; otherwise, you leave the field to critics. A permissible leak is straightforward, factual, in context. Understand that a good reporter will not run with just what you tell him but will use the leak to pry out more information elsewhere to round out the story. It is impermissible to leak if the information is false or misleading, would slander someone, or would be personally self-serving. It would also probably get the leaker into trouble once the checks have been made and the leak proven false.

• **Yell About Mistakes.** Journalists, being human and fallible, make mistakes, some more than others. Do not let them pass. If mistakes are allowed to stand, they will be compounded by later stories and in data banks. More important, editors and reporters learn no lessons when mistakes are allowed to go by. The first step is to ask the reporter to run a correction, either in a place set aside for that or in the next day's article if it is a running story. The correction is more likely to be put into context in a story than in the corrections column. If the reporter refuses, go to his boss. If that doesn't work, go to the top editor. If you are still not satisfied, call up the competitors. There's little one reporter would rather do than catch his competitor in a mistake.

• **To Pool or Not to Pool?** After the ruckus over the exclusion of the press from Grenada in 1983, the Pentagon organized a press pool that was to be called out to cover contingency operations. From the beginning, the concept was flawed by basic differences in the way the press and the Pentagon looked at the pool. Those flaws surfaced in Panama in 1989 and left serious doubts as to whether the pool should survive. Most journalists see a pool as a temporary expedient when access is limited. For example, a small pool travels with the President on Air Force One because the entire White House press corps can't fit aboard. A pool is set up for a single mission. The task of the members is to gather information and to pass it on to the rest of the press as soon as possible. Most important, the pool self-destructs as soon as full coverage begins.

From the Pentagon's perspective, however, the pool has been a way to limit access, to control coverage, and to minimize the burden of having reporters around. Communications, the lifeblood of correspondents in the field, have been largely ignored. All of that came out in Panama, where the pool was a miserable failure. When it was over, Fred Hoffman, the former Associated Press correspondent in the Pentagon and then Deputy Assistant Secretary of Defense for Public Affairs in the Reagan Administration, was asked to determine why the pool had failed.

His report was scathing. Mr. Hoffman laid much of the blame on Mr. Pete Williams, the Assistant Secretary of Defense for Public Affairs, for "less than effective leadership and performance."[8] There was no public affairs plan when the operation was mounted, the pool was called out too late to cover the decisive assaults, and unit commanders in the field "had no idea" of what the pool was all about.

Mr. Hoffman said military leaders played no part in the decision to delay activating the pool and quoted General Maxwell R. Thurman, the SOUTHCOM commander, as saying: "I think we made a mistake by not having some of the press pool in with the 18th Airborne Corps so they could move with the troops."[9] Pentagon officials said later that General Powell, the Chairman of the Joint Chiefs of Staff, was unhappy with the pool arrangement in Panama and had taken a strong hand in seeking to put things right. But when Operation Desert Shield in Saudi Arabia was mounted in 1990, the Pentagon delayed again in calling out the pool because the Saudi government was not keen on press coverage. After that was straightened out, the pool worked fairly well until its dissolution when full coverage began.

Conclusion: The entire concept should be reexamined from top to bottom. Mr. Hoffman suggested such scrutiny in his report, but the response from the Pentagon was lukewarm and the prospects for the pool ever working are dim.

▪ **Forget Media Days.** The "media days" held by the war colleges and intermediate military schools in which reporters are invited to discuss military-press relations have been, with rare exceptions, a waste of time. Officers posture by wrapping themselves in the flag and journalists do likewise by standing on the pedestal of the First Amendment. The sessions end in mutual bloodletting with no communication, no one's mind changed, and more ill will when the antagonists are pulled apart.

Moreover, the wrong people are talking to each other. Lieutenant colonels and commanders on one side and frontline reporters and television producers on the other can't do much to improve matters. The people who need to get into this struggle are generals and admirals and senior editors and producers, the people with the authority to change things.

A suggested substitute for media days would be to have a service chief invite ten or a dozen top editors and producers to Washington for a day. The chief, the vice chief, and the senior staff, including the chief of public affairs, would air their concerns about the press and television in a calm and professional manner. They would then invite the senior journalists to bring up their problems in covering the military services.

To follow up, the commandant of the service's war college could invite managing and assistant managing editors for a similar session at Carlisle Barracks, Maxwell AFB, or Newport. Still another follow-up would have the service's chief of public affairs meet with press and television bureau chiefs in Washington. The whole process could be repeated every year or two.

▪ **Educate Officers.** In a moment of pleasantry before beginning an interview, a three-star general asked a reporter whether he got paid by the word or the article. The general was surprised to learn that staff journalists are paid salaries, just like soldiers, and that they are paid whether they write that day or not. Many military people haven't the foggiest notion of how the press and television operate and why. (In fairness, neither do some journalists.) Little is taught about the press in the military academies or ROTC programs and even less as the officer progresses through his military education.

To rectify this situation, the services might insert a three-hour block of instruction into courses for junior officers. It would cover the First Amendment, the press as a diverse institution, and what a public affairs officer is. At mid-level courses, a four-hour block would expand on the role of the press in peace and war, on differences in dealing with the press and television, and on how to talk to a reporter. Handling classified or sensitive information vis-à-vis the press would get particular attention.

At the war colleges, instruction would include an eight-hour block on political issues, practice sessions in working with reporters, and case studies in which officers did well or stubbed their toes. Lastly, generals-to-be would get some constructive indoctrination on press relations when they attend charm school before having their stars pinned on, certainly more than a few hours coaching on the tactics and gamesmanship of dealing with reporters.

• **Educate Journalists.** Defense industry executives who assembled at the Industrial College of the Armed Forces in Washington were wailing the usual litany about press coverage. Finally a reporter asked how many of them had ever invited the editor of the local paper out to the plant for coffee. Only a half-dozen raised their hands.

Since military officers and defense executives do little to educate the journalists assigned to cover them, their first encounters often come only after all hell has broken loose. Then the executives or officers are confronted with a bunch of demanding, competitive, and often rude strangers. How much better it would be if a post commander or chief of staff invited the edtior for lunch to talk over what was going on at Camp Swampy and to learn what the editor had on his mind—all before a crisis; or if the public affairs officer had invited a reporter out for a day of briefings and informal looking around, with neither expecting a story to come out of the visit.

That sort of education generates more understanding of military life, makes for better stories, and, when the crunch comes, produces a journalist willing to listen before rushing to judgment in print or on the tube. Such educational sessions are best done one-on-one or with a small group of compatible people. A large gaggle of reporters from newspapers, television, radio, and the trade magazines usually doesn't work because the briefings get to be canned, a schedule must be followed, and everyone has a different set of questions.

• **Support Public Affairs Officers.** Journalists are sometimes asked which service has the best PAOs. Truth, and a sense of survival because a correspondent must work with them all, dictates this answer: Each service has its share of first-class, competent, dedicated public affairs officers. Unhappily, each service also has its share of time-servers who go through the mechanical motions of public affairs.

The most important element in the relationship between a journalist and a PAO is the policy of the PAO's commander. A commander with an open attitude communicates that tone to his subordinates and enables the PAO to do his job. A commander who wants a palace guard will get it, and with it, most likely, a bundle of bad press clippings. The commander should demand the assignment of a competent PAO and listen to him as with any other staff officer. Equally important, when things beyond the PAO's reach go wrong, and they will, the commander must protect him against wrath from above, just as he would protect another staff officer.

A final observation: The Army and Marine Corps require young officers to spend time with troops before becoming public affairs officers. That seasons them and gives them credibility. The Navy and Air Force, in contrast, make PAOs out of young officers who, while they may be fine people, lack the feel of the deck or the flight line. They are too inexperienced to do much more than pass out press releases.

Notes

1. Dwight D. Eisenhower, *Crusade in Europe* (Garden City, N.Y.: Doubleday and Company, 1948), p. 299.

2. Ibid., p. 300.

3. Liz Trotta, Seminar Transcript, Gannett Center for Media Studies, Columbia University, New York, N.Y., 11 April 1990, p. 40.

4. Elie Abel, "Leaking: Who Does It? Who Benefits? At What Cost?" Twentieth Century Fund Paper (New York, N.Y.: Priority Press, 1987), p. 68.

5. As quoted in "Gen. Powell Says NSC Again 'Moral Operation,' " *The Washington Post*, 28 October 1988, p. A3.

6. As quoted in the *Los Angeles Times*, 16 September 1990, p. M3.

7. Robert B. Sims, *The Pentagon Reporters* (Washington: National Defense Univ. Press, 1983), p. 150.

8. Fred S. Hoffman, "Review of the Panama Pool Deployment, December 1989," Memorandum for Correspondents, The Pentagon, Washington, D.C., 20 March 1990, (reprinted in chapter 8 of this volume).

9. Ibid. SOUTHCOM is Southern Command.

This article originally appeared in the March 1991 issue of *Parameters*.

About the Contributors

MR. PETER BRAESTRUP is senior editor of the Library of Congress. He received his B.A. from Yale University in 1951 and was commissioned as a second lieutenant in the Marine Corps, serving until 1953. During the Korean War, he was wounded while participating in the defense of Outpost Reno. Following release from the Marines, he joined *Time* magazine as a staff writer and has pursued a career in journalism from that time. Other major news organs he has served are the *New York Herald Tribune, The New York Times*, and *The Washington Post*. He began coverage of the Indo-China war from Bangkok in 1966–68 for the *Times*, and became Saigon bureau chief for the *Post* in January 1968, just prior to Tet, remaining in that post until 1969. In 1972, he returned to Vietnam to cover Hanoi's Easter offensive. Mr. Braestrup was editor of the *Wilson Quarterly* from 1975 to 1989. He is the author of *Big Story: How the American Press and Television Reported and Interpreted the Crisis of Tet 1968 in Vietnam and Washington* (1977) and the Background Paper for *Battle Lines: Report of the Twentieth Century Fund Task Force on the Military and the Media* (1985).

COLONEL LLOYD J. MATTHEWS, U.S. Army (Ret.), is editor of *Parameters: U.S. Army War College Quarterly.* He holds a B.S. from the U.S. Military Academy, an M.A. from Harvard University, and a Ph.D. from the University of Virginia, and is a graduate of the Army War College. Colonel Matthews has been connected with *Parameters* for over 13 years as associate editor or editor. He served in Vietnam in 1964–65 as an adviser to South Vietnamese forces and commanded a battalion at Ford Ord, Calif., prior to his appointment as professor of English at West Point. He was the associate dean of the Military Academy from 1981 to 1984. Colonel Matthews is co-editor of four previous Brassey's volumes—*Parameters of War* (1987), *Assessing the Vietnam War* (1987), *The Challenge of Military Leadership* (1989), and *The Parameters of Military Ethics* (1989).

■ ■ ■ ■ ■ ■

143

AMBASSADOR L. PAUL BREMER III, now retired from the Senior Foreign Service, is a graduate of Yale (B.A., 1963) and Harvard (M.B.A., 1966), and holds a certificate from the Institut d'Etudes Politiques in Paris (1964). From entry into the Foreign Service in 1966, his foreign postings included Afghanistan, Malawi, Norway, and the Netherlands, to the latter of which he was U.S. Ambassador. Home assignments included a two-year stint as executive secretary and special assistant to the Secretary of State. He was U.S. Ambassador at Large for Counter-Terrorism from 1986 to 1988. Ambassador Bremer is presently managing director of Kissinger Associates, Inc., in New York.

MR. JOSEPH H. EWING has worked in the U.S. Civil Service, principally as an Army historian. The newly revealed letters by General William Tecumseh Sherman were written to Mr. Ewing's great grandfather, Thomas Ewing, and to his grandfather, Philemon B. Ewing. Mr. Ewing is the author of *29, Let's Go! A History of the 29th Infantry Division in World War II* (1948). He served in the 29th Division during the war as a platoon leader in Company G of the 175th Infantry in Germany.

MR. RICHARD HALLORAN received his A.B. from Dartmouth College in 1951 and enlisted in the Army the following year. He was commissioned through OCS, and served with the 82nd Airborne Division at Fort Bragg, N.C., and with military advisory groups in Japan, Okinawa, Korea, Vietnam, and Taiwan. Returning to school, he earned an M.A. from the University of Michigan and was awarded a Ford Foundation Fellowship in Advanced International Reporting at Columbia University. A career journalist, he has worked for *Business Week, The Washington Post,* and *The New York Times.* He was with *The Times* from 1969 to 1989, covering military affairs for the last ten years of that period. Mr. Halloran's four books include *To Arm a Nation: Rebuilding America's Endangered Defenses* (1986) and *Serving America: Prospects for the Volunteer Force* (1988). He is presently director of special projects for the East-West Center in Honolulu, responsible for programs in journalism and topical research on issues of America's relations with Asia.

DR. WILLIAM M. HAMMOND is a historian at the U.S. Army Center of Military History in Washington, D.C. He is a graduate of the Catholic University of America, where he received the S.T.B., M.A., and Ph.D. degrees. Dr. Hammond has lectured widely in the Army's educational system and has taught at the University of Maryland (Baltimore County) and at Trinity College. He is the author of a two-volume study of the military's relations with the news media during the Vietnam War. The first volume, titled *The U.S. Army in Vietnam: The Military and the Media, 1962–1968* (Washington: Army Center of Military History), was published in 1988. The second, covering the Nixon years, is in progress.

MR. FRED S. HOFFMAN served in the U.S. Army during World War II and attended Boston University. He was a Washington reporter and editor for over 39 years, including nearly a quarter of a century as the Associated Press's senior military writer. Prior to his retirement at the end of 1989, he was the Principal Deputy Assistant Secretary of Defense for Public Affairs, a position he held for over five years. Upon retirement, he was asked by the Assistant Secretary of Defense for Public Affairs to review the experience of the press pool covering Operation Just Cause (Panama), launched in December 1989, and to make appropriate recommendations. His March 1990 report was based upon two months of interviews with more than 50 persons involved, including civilian and military officials, staff and pool escort officers, troop commanders, and newsmen from the pool.

MR. WILLIAM A. RUSHER retired at the end of 1988 after 31 years as publisher of *National Review*. He had earlier been a practicing lawyer for nine years, including seven and a half years with Wall Street's largest law firm and 17 months as associate counsel to the U.S. Senate's Internal Security Subcommittee. In addition to a syndicated column, he has written *The Rise of the Right* (1984) and *The Coming Battle for the Media: Curbing the Power of the Media Elite* (1988).

DR. SAM C. SARKESIAN received his B.A. from The Citadel and his M.A. and Ph.D. from Columbia University. He is currently professor of political science at Loyola University of Chicago and was formerly chairman of the Inter-University Seminar on Armed Forces and Society. He served for over 20 years as an enlisted man and officer in the U.S. Army, with service in Germany, Korea, and Vietnam, including duty with Special Forces, airborne, and infantry units. Dr. Sarkesian has produced some 15 books, his latest effort being *The U.S. Army in a New Security Era* (co-editor; 1990).

LIEUTENANT GENERAL BERNARD E. TRAINOR, U.S. Marine Corps (Ret.), is director of the national security program at the Kennedy School of Government, Harvard University. He retired from the Marine Corps in 1985 and served as the military correspondent for *The New York Times* until the spring of 1990. General Trainor was a highly decorated officer who held combat commands in both the Korean and Vietnam wars. He is a graduate of Holy Cross College and holds a master's degree in history from the University of Colorado. He attended the Marine Corps Command and Staff College and the Air War College. In his work for *The Times*, General Trainor covered military matters at home and abroad and provided on-the-scene analysis of conflicts throughout the Third World.

COLONEL JOHN D. WAGHELSTEIN, U.S. Army (Ret.), is a professor in the Operations Department of the Naval War College in Newport, R.I. He holds a B.A. in history from Western Maryland College (Westminster), an M.A. in international relations from Cornell University, and a Ph.D. in history from Temple University, and is a graduate of the Army War College. He served two tours in Vietnam, three in Panama, and one in Bolivia, and was commander of the U.S. Army Element, Military Group, in El Salvador in 1982–83. Later, he was commander of the 7th Special Forces Group at Ft. Bragg, N.C., and an instructor in the Department of Military Strategy, Planning, and Operations of the Army War College.

LIEUTENANT COLONEL BARRY E. WILLEY, an infantry officer in the U.S. Army, graduated from the Military Academy in 1972. He later earned an M.A. degree in journalism from Indiana University. As public affairs officer for the 82nd Airborne Division in October 1983, Colonel Willey participated in Operation Urgent Fury in Grenada and coordinated military support for the media pools permitted on the island. He was a military escort officer for the media pool during the first transit of reflagged Kuwaiti tankers when the supertanker *Bridgeton* hit a mine in July 1987, and also during the U.S.-Iranian Gulf hostilities of April 1988 when U.S. forces attacked Iranian oil platforms and frigates. After a tour as media relations officer for U.S. Central Command, McDill Air Force Base, Fla., he became executive officer of the 2nd Brigade, 24th Infantry Division, which deployed to Saudi Arabia in the fall of 1990.